30 Day Whole Food Challenge

Healthy And Delicious Whole Food Recipes For Easy Weight Loss

Table of Contents

Introduction

In this book you will find over a hundred recipes that are 100% organic, easy on the budget and friendly on the waistline. Each weekly meal plan is a variety of whole food recipes ranging from soups and salads to chicken dishes, roasted meats, baked goods, and many others. It is guaranteed that the ingredients used in each dish are clean, chemical-free, and devoid of artificial flavors and preservatives.

The term *"whole foods"* refers to ingredients that are organic and closest to their natural state, which means they have either sprouted from the ground or have been sourced from animals. These foods contain healthy doses of vitamins and nutrients such as carbohydrates, protein, fat, fiber, natural sugars, and sodium. Fruits, vegetables, lean protein, grains, eggs, dairy, oils, seeds and nuts are the main components of a whole food diet.

Whole foods provide the human body with numerous health benefits such as lower health numbers, a stronger immune system, and healthier digestion. However, another major contribution of whole foods is its fat-burning properties, making it a perfect weight loss partner. A regular intake of organic dishes helps boost metabolism, raises energy levels, and triggers ketosis, a fat-burning process that results in weight loss.

This book provides us with basic know-how about whole foods, including their role in long-term weight loss and how eating them is a much better option than eating processed, unhealthy ingredients. You will likewise find tips, a whole foods list, and recipes that will guide you on your 30-day whole food challenge.

Let's begin the journey.

Chapter 1: Whole Foods: Cornerstone of Weight Loss

"Don't eat anything your great-great grandmother wouldn't recognize as food. There are a great many food-like items in the supermarket your ancestors wouldn't recognize as food...stay away from these."

Michael Pollan
American author and organic food activist

A colorful and nutritious diet composed of whole, organic foods is the cornerstone of long-term weight management. Essentially, what we put inside our mouths ends up in our waistline, arms, and thighs. Thus, it is important for us to be mindful of our daily food choices, most especially if we are aiming to lose a few inches around the body.

Popular weight loss programs such as Paleo, Atkins, Low-Carb, and South Beach share a common objective: to promote whole foods as a means to achieve weight loss goals and optimum health. All these programs support the proliferation of organic eating in today's society with the hopes of eliminating the unhealthy effects of artificial sugars, manufactured snacks, and fast food.

If you are one of those people who constantly feel sick or are suffering from obesity, diabetes, and other lifestyle diseases, it is important for you to know that you can experience healthy and rapid weight loss by eating whole foods. Transitioning to a whole food lifestyle is unlike that of adopting a new diet: it is simply eating food that is natural, healthy and genetically familiar to the human body.

Whole Foods: A Basic Guide

Whole foods are plant and animal-based ingredients that have not been genetically-modified or artificially-produced. These foods are closest to their natural state and are packed with vitamins, minerals, and phytochemicals which fight disease and strengthen immunity.

In addition to being nutritious, whole foods are usually low in calories but contain healthy amounts of carbohydrates, fats, protein, sodium, and natural sugar. The perfect ratio between these nutrients is what triggers faster metabolism, high energy levels, and regulated health numbers, which in turn leads to weight loss and a better quality of life.

Some examples of whole foods are the following:

- Vegetables

- Fruits

- Whole wheat and whole-grain foods

- Dairy and eggs

- Meats and poultry

- Nuts and seeds

- Healthy oils

- Herbs and spices

How Processed Food Promotes Weight Gain

One of the major causes of weight gain and disease in today's society is the daily intake of high-carb, processed food. Food manufacturers create cheap, tasty and visually-appealing food items that contain high amounts of salt, sugar, starch and empty carbohydrates. These levels are harmful enough to alter the body's cell production and hormonal activities.

Hence, people who are used to a diet of salty snacks, sweets, and refined starches usually find themselves feeling sick, lethargic, or not wanting to engage in physical activity even after having a spike of energy from drinking a chocolate milkshake or eating a slice of pizza.

Consequently, a sedentary lifestyle brought about by an unhealthy diet will result in weight gain and an over-production of fat cells. If uncontrolled, unhealthy eating may even lead to obesity, diabetes and other health problems such as heart disease, hypertension and chronic pain.

Why Whole Foods Naturally Result to Weight Loss

On the other end of the spectrum, people who consume whole foods daily are healthier, leaner, and more energetic. Eating salads, vegetable soup, lean protein, healthy oils and fruits have helped them manage their weight and sustain high energy levels for fat-burning activities such as yoga or running.

In general, whole foods contain low amounts of carbohydrates and calories which make them ideal for weight loss. However, organic fruits and vegetables are loaded with fiber, protein, and good fat. Consumption of cleaner foods may have little or no effect on one's weight but it does help build a healthier body both inside and out.

Moreover, the healthy fats from oils such as nuts, olive oil, coconuts, and avocadoes do not turn into visceral fat. These fats are transformed into fuel and burned off easily. This process, called ketosis, is what makes eating whole foods a major factor in losing weight.

Now that you know how whole foods boost weight loss, it's time to challenge yourself by starting a 30-day whole food challenge. The process may seem difficult at first, but the results will be worth it in the end.

Chapter 2: Strategies to Start a Whole Food Lifestyle

"Take care of your body.
It's the only place you have to live."

Jim Rohn
American author and motivational speaker

The 30-day whole food challenge may prove difficult in the beginning, most especially if you have been used to eating sweets, snacks and other unhealthy meals. You may even start questioning yourself on why you want to embrace this lifestyle given that a lot of your favorite foods are barred from the whole foods list.

However, if you are serious about achieving your fitness goals, it is important for you to fully commit to eating whole, unprocessed foods. Luckily, this book will help you transition to a weight-friendly diet as it contains more than a hundred whole food recipes that are flavorful, economical, and easy to prepare.

If you are ready for a new chapter in your life, here are a few strategies that will help you start a clean, whole food lifestyle:

Shop for Whole Foods

Whole foods generally consist of fresh and dried produce, meats, seafood, oils, dairy, and grains. While planning your meals, create a comprehensive grocery list of organic foods. Once you are in the grocery or at your local farmers market, purchase the items you wrote on your list and make sure that you stick to it. Ask the produce manager to help you select high-quality ingredients and the best cuts of protein for your recipes.

The following chapter contains a complete grocery list of whole foods that you can refer to while shopping.

Cook Whole Foods

Once you have your ingredients, try cooking the recipes one meal at a time. As you follow the recipes in this book, you will find yourself becoming more at ease with combining organic ingredients and making healthy food substitutions.

Eat More Whole Foods

Once you have cooked your first whole food dish, try it for yourself or serve it to your family. You will realize that whole food dishes are not only quick and easy to prepare, but they taste good as well. Eating healthy should not be boring: you have a colorful array of organic condiments, herbs and spices that will enhance the flavors of your dish.

Drink Whole

An equally important part of embracing a whole foods lifestyle is to cleanse your palate with natural, sugar-free, and chemical-free drinks such as water, natural fruit juices, and herbal teas. These drinks contain zero calories and will not add inches to the waistline. Moreover, guzzling these natural fluids regulates digestion, speeds up metabolism and rejuvenates the body.

Care for Your Whole Self

Self-care is important while in the process of losing weight. Whole foods will help your body become lighter and leaner, but it is important to do other activities that will help keep you focused and motivated. Activities such as exercise, yoga, meditation, and reading will help take away stress and enable you to become more comfortable with your body even as you are transitioning to a better version of yourself.

Now that you have basic know-how on how to begin a healthier way of eating, the succeeding chapter will show you a whole foods grocery list which will serve as your guide while choosing the right ingredients for your everyday meals.

Chapter 3: Ultimate Grocery List of Whole Foods

"Your diet is a bank account.
Good food choices are good investments."

Bethenny Frankel
American author, chef and TV personality

You should fill your kitchen with a vast and colorful variety of whole foods. Apart from their health-giving nutrients, whole foods provide naturally delicious flavors that will satisfy even the pickiest palate.

Below is a complete list of whole foods:

<u>Vegetables</u> – Kale, spinach, lettuce, cabbage, collard greens, Bok Choy, Swiss chard, arugula, asparagus, eggplant, turnip, sweet potato, celery, squash, cucumber, zucchini, jicama, rutabaga, beet, tomato, Brussels sprouts, parsnip, bell pepper, broccoli, cauliflower, carrot, okra, onions, chayote, green onions, shallots, mushrooms

<u>Fresh/Dried Fruits</u> – Banana, mango, orange, apple, pineapple, apricot, peach, berries, avocado, melon, kiwi, lemon, lime, papaya, olives, raisins, cranberries, cherries

<u>Meats & Poultry</u> – Whole and ground chicken, turkey, beef and pork, lamb, duck, venison, bison, low-sodium bacon

Seafood – Sea bass, salmon, mackerel, sardines, anchovies, tilapia, cod, cream dory, catfish, herring, trout, squid, shrimp, prawn, clams, mussels, oysters, scallops, crab meat, canned tuna

Oils – Olive oil, coconut oil, organic ghee, avocado oil, grape seed oil, sunflower oil, macadamia oil, walnut oil, organic unsalted butter

Raw Nuts & Seeds – Quinoa, flaxseeds, chia seeds, sunflower seeds, pumpkin seeds, sesame seeds, poppy seeds, almonds, walnuts, hazelnuts, pistachios, pecans, pine nuts, chestnuts, Brazil nuts

Raw/Dried Beans – String beans, sugar snap peas, mung beans, black beans, kidney beans, chickpeas, navy beans, pinto beans, tofu

Dairy – Raw milk, almond milk, rice milk, soy milk, coconut milk, coconut cream, cottage cheese, whole Parmesan cheese, goat cheese, ricotta cheese, plain yoghurt, Greek yoghurt, eggs

Grains – Quinoa, brown rice, plain oats, barley, sorghum, amaranth, millet, spelt, rye, buckwheat, bulgur, whole wheat bread, pasta and tortillas

Fresh/Dried Herbs – Oregano, basil, dill, thyme, sage, rosemary, parsley, tarragon, bay leaves, chive, mint, coriander

Spices – Sea salt, chili peppers, chili powder, pepper flakes, garlic, ginger, cayenne pepper, paprika, garlic powder, onion powder, turmeric, black peppercorns, cardamom, fennel seeds, cumin, coriander, cinnamon, nutmeg, allspice, lemon pepper seasoning, white pepper, star anise

<u>Flours, Baking Ingredients, and Sweeteners</u> – Raw honey, maple syrup, coconut sugar, dates, tapioca flour, almond flour, arrowroot flour, coconut flour, whole wheat flour, grated coconut, cocoa powder, dark chocolate, vanilla extract, almond extract, peppermint extract, baking powder, baking soda

<u>Condiments & Spreads</u> – Vinegar, coconut aminos, organic mayonnaise, Dijon mustard, nut butter, homemade jams

<u>Others</u> – Homemade chicken/beef/vegetable stock, unflavored gelatin, black coffee, all-natural and unsweetened fruit/vegetable juice, herbal tea, water

Now that you have a comprehensive food guide, it's time to try out the recipes in the succeeding chapters. Each breakfast, lunch, dinner, and snack recipe contains a delicious mixture of whole flavors that will help you enjoy your weight loss journey.

Enjoy cooking!

Chapter 4: Week 1 Recipes

DAY 1

BREAKFAST

Strawberry & Peach Pudding

Ingredients:

- 1 cup chopped strawberries

- ¾ cup chia seeds

- 1 tablespoon raw honey

- ¾ cup chopped peaches

- 3 cups almond milk

Directions:

1. Combine almond milk, honey, and chia seeds in a bowl. Mix well and let it sit for 10 minutes. After 10 minutes, whisk the mixture then place it in the fridge for 2 hours.

2. Remove the chia mixture from the fridge. Add in the chopped strawberries and peaches. Mix the pudding well. Serve immediately.

3. This recipe yields 4 servings.

LUNCH

Slow Cooker Vegetable Soup

Ingredients:

- 3 cups diced tomatoes

- 1 medium carrot, peeled and chopped

- 2 celery stalks, chopped

- 2 cups cubed squash

- 1 medium zucchini, peeled and chopped

- 1 white onion, minced

- 1 cup broccoli florets

- 5 cups homemade chicken stock

- ½ teaspoon sea salt

- ½ teaspoon garlic powder

- Dash of ground black pepper

Directions:

1. Combine tomatoes, carrots, celery, squash, zucchini, onion, broccoli, garlic powder, salt, and pepper in a 4-quart slow cooker. Mix well.

2. Pour in the chicken stock then cover the pot. Set the temperature to high and cook for 4 hours.

3. Stir the soup and serve immediately.

4. This recipe yields 7-8 servings.

DINNER

Oven-Roasted Seabass

Ingredients:

- 2 medium sea bass fillets

- ½ cup olive oil

- ½ cup parsley

- 1 ½ teaspoons sea salt

- ½ teaspoon minced garlic

- 1 tablespoon almonds

- 1 tablespoon fresh lemon juice

- 1 tablespoon coconut oil

- 1 teaspoon ground black pepper

Directions:

1. To make pesto, combine parsley, almonds, olive oil, garlic, pepper and a teaspoon of lemon juice in a food processor. Mix until the pesto is smooth and pasty. Set aside.

2. Preheat the oven to 400°F and line a baking dish with parchment paper.

3. Place the sea bass on the baking dish with the skin facing down. Rub the olive oil and remaining lemon juice on the fillets and place them in the oven. Bake for 8-10 minutes.

4. Remove the fish from the oven. Spoon the pesto on the fillets and place them back in the oven. Bake this for 5 minutes then turn off the heat.

5. Let the fillets cool at room temperature for 5 minutes. Serve immediately.

6. This recipe yields 2 servings,

SNACK

Cinnamon Apple Slices

Ingredients:

- 5 apples, cored and peeled

- 1 tablespoon maple syrup

- 1 tablespoon grated lemon zest

- ½ teaspoon cinnamon powder

- ¼ cup lemon juice

- ½ cup apple juice

Directions:

1. Preheat the oven to 250°F and prepare a round baking dish.

2. Slice the apples into thin rounds and arrange it on the dish, overlapping one another. Pour the apple juice, maple syrup and lemon juice on the apple slices.

3. Sprinkle lemon zest and cinnamon powder on top. Bake the apples in the oven for 8-10 minutes or until the apples are tender.

4. Serve the apples in small plates and serve immediately.

5. This recipe yields 5 servings.

DAY 2

BREAKFAST

Banana & Avocado Smoothie

Ingredients:

- 1 whole avocado, pitted and peeled

- 3 bananas, peeled

- 1 cup spinach leaves

- 1 ½ cup coconut milk

- ½ cup flaxseed meal

Directions:

1. Scoop out the flesh from the avocado and place it in a blender. Mix in the bananas, spinach, flaxseed and coconut milk.

2. Process the ingredients together for 30 seconds. Pour into glasses and serve.

3. This recipe yields 2 servings.

LUNCH

Spiced Turkey Meatballs

Ingredients:

- 450 grams ground turkey

- 1 large egg, whisked

- 1 sweet onion, minced

- 1 cup chopped green onions

- ½ red bell pepper, minced

- ½ cup almond flour

- 1 teaspoon cayenne pepper

- ½ teaspoon cumin

- ½ teaspoon sea salt

- Dash of ground black pepper

Directions:

1. Preheat the oven to 350°F and line a baking sheet with parchment paper.

2. Combine ground turkey, egg, onions, bell pepper and almond flour in a bowl and knead with your hands. Season the meatball mixture with salt, pepper, cumin and cayenne pepper. Knead until well-combined.

3. Use your hand to form 1-inch balls from the turkey mixture. Arrange the balls on the baking sheet and bake for 30 minutes.

4. Let the meatballs cool at room temperature for 10 minutes then serve immediately.

5. This recipe yields 8 servings.

DINNER

Hearty Sweet Potato Chowder

Ingredients:

- 500 grams sweet potatoes, peeled and diced

- 2 medium carrots, diced

- 1 cup cremini mushrooms, chopped

- 1 small red onion, minced

- 1 tablespoon minced garlic

- 1 tablespoon minced ginger

- 2 teaspoons fresh thyme

- 3 cups homemade chicken stock

- ¼ cup coconut milk

- 1 teaspoon olive oil

- Pinch of sea salt and ground black pepper

Directions:

1. Heat the olive oil in a soup pot over medium-high flame. Add garlic, ginger and onions and sauté for 5 minutes.

2. Add in carrots, sweet potatoes, mushrooms and thyme. Season with salt and pepper then cook the vegetables for 5 minutes.

3. Pour in chicken stock and cover the pot. Let the chowder boil then lower the flame to medium. Simmer for 10 minutes or until the sweet potatoes are tender.

4. Once the chowder is ready, turn off the flame and use an immersion blender to process the soup until creamy. Pour the chowder in a large soup bowl then mix in the coconut milk before serving.

5. This recipe yields 5 servings.

SNACK

Coconut Almond Squares

Ingredients:

- 1 cup desiccated coconut

- 4 tablespoons almond butter

- ½ cup ground almonds

- ½ cup sunflower seeds

- ¼ cup ground walnuts

- 3 tablespoons raw honey

- ½ teaspoon sesame oil

- Pinch of sea salt

Directions:

1. Preheat the oven to 350°F and grease a square 8 x 8 baking pan with sesame oil.

2. Combine coconut, almond butter, almonds, sunflower seeds, walnuts, raw honey and salt in a blender and pulse until smooth. Pour the mixture into the pan and spread evenly.

3. Bake the mixture in the oven for 15 minutes. Remove the dish from the oven and let it cool for 10 minutes. Slice into squares and refrigerate.

4. This recipe yields 4 servings.

DAY 3

BREAKFAST

Early Riser's Banana Boats

Ingredients:

- 4 tablespoons pureed blueberries

- 4 bananas, peeled and halved

- ½ cup chopped almonds

- 2 cups cottage cheese

- Pinch of sea salt

Directions:

1. Prepare 4 small oval dishes.

2. Place 2 banana slices in a bowl. Use a spoon to scoop a quarter of the cottage cheese then place it on the banana.

3. Place a tablespoon of the pureed blueberries on top of the cottage cheese then sprinkle almonds and sea salt on top. Do the same procedure for the remaining ingredients.

4. This recipe yields 4 servings.

LUNCH

Pan-Fried Spicy Chicken Thighs

Ingredients:

- 10 chicken thighs, deboned

- 2 tablespoons lime juice

- 1 teaspoon lime zest

- 1 tablespoon fresh rosemary

- 2 tablespoons coconut oil

- 2 tablespoons olive oil

- 1 tablespoon minced garlic

- 1 teaspoon sea salt

- ½ teaspoon lemon pepper seasoning

Directions:

1. Place chicken thighs on a flat surface and pound with a meat mallet. Transfer the chicken to a large bowl then season with olive oil, lime juice, lime zest, lemon pepper seasoning, rosemary, garlic and sea salt. Place it in the fridge for 3 hours.

2. After 3 hours, take the chicken out of the fridge then place them on a large colander to drain the liquids completely.

3. Heat the coconut oil in a pan over medium-high flame. Fry the chicken thighs skin-side down on the pan for 8 minutes or until the skin turns golden brown.

4. Flip the chicken thighs over then cook the meat side for 5 minutes. Place the cooked thighs on a rack to drain excess oil.

5. Let the chicken thighs cool for 10 minutes then serve immediately.

This recipe yields 5 servings.

DINNER

Arugula and Mackerel Salad

Ingredients:

- 4 cups arugula or rocket leaves, washed and drained

- 3 hard-boiled eggs, peeled

- 200 grams mackerel fillets

- 1 ½ cups string bean, cut into 1-inch slices

- 1 small avocado, halved, peeled and pitted

- 3 tablespoons olive oil

- ½ teaspoon sea salt

- 1 teaspoon Dijon mustard

- 2 tablespoons lemon juice

- Pinch of ground black pepper

Directions:

1. Cut the avocado and eggs into thin slices. Set aside.

2. Boil the string beans in water for 5 minutes. Once the beans are tender, turn off the flame then drain the water completely. Set aside.

3. Combine pepper, lemon juice, mustard, salt, and 1 tablespoon of the olive oil in a salad bowl. Whisk the ingredients until a smooth dressing is produced. Add in the arugula leaves and string beans then toss. Chill in the fridge for 1 hour.

4. Heat the remaining oil in a pan over medium-high flame. Fry the mackerel fillets until both sides are golden brown.

5. To assemble the salad, take out the chilled greens from the fridge. Arrange the avocado slices, eggs and mackerel on top then serve immediately.

6. This recipe yields 3 servings.

SNACK

Cherry Hazelnut Bark

Ingredients:

- 5 tablespoons cocoa powder

- 3 tablespoons raw honey

- 4 tablespoons coconut oil, melted

- 1 teaspoon sea salt

- 3 tablespoons cherries, pitted and chopped

- 1 cup hazelnuts, roasted, peeled and chopped

- ½ teaspoon vanilla extract

Directions:

1. Combine cocoa powder and coconut oil in a bowl and mix well. Add in honey, vanilla and salt then stir. Pour the chocolate mixture into a small baking dish.

2. Sprinkle chopped hazelnuts and cherries on the chocolate mixture. Place the dish in the freezer for 2 hours.

3. Unmold the chocolate bark from the baking dish and lightly tap it to form big chocolate shards. Store the chocolate in an airtight container.

4. This recipe yields 6 servings.

DAY 4

BREAKFAST

Maple Quinoa Cereal

Ingredients:

- 4 cups quinoa flakes

- 4 tablespoons almond butter

- 3 tablespoons maple syrup

- 4 cups almond milk

Directions:

1. Preheat the oven to 350°F and line a baking dish with parchment paper.

2. Combine almond butter and syrup in a bowl and whisk them together. Pour in the quinoa flakes and stir to combine. Pour the mixture into the baking dish.

3. Bake the cereal in the oven for 12-15 minutes, making sure to stir every 6 minutes. Remove the cereal from the oven and let it cool at room temperature.

4. To serve the cereal, place equal portions of the cereal into the bowls and pour a cup of almond milk per serving.

5. This recipe yields 4 servings.

LUNCH

Almond-Crusted Catfish with Peppers

Ingredients:

- 4 frozen catfish fillets, thawed

- 1 cup ground almonds

- ¼ cup flaxseed meal

- ¼ cup almond flour

- ½ teaspoon cayenne pepper

- ½ teaspoon sea salt

- 1 large egg, whisked

- 1 tablespoon water

- 1 red bell pepper, deseeded and julienned

- 1 yellow bell pepper, deseeded and julienned

- 1 green bell pepper, deseeded and julienned

- 2 teaspoons olive oil

- Pinch of garlic powder

Directions:

1. Preheat the oven to 425°F and lightly grease a baking pan with cooking spray.

2. Whisk together egg and water in a bowl. Set aside.

3. In a separate bowl, combine ground almonds, flaxseed, sea salt and cayenne pepper. Set aside.

4. Dip the catfish in the almond flour, followed by the egg mixture. Finally, dredge the fish in the almond and flaxseed breading then place it on the baking pan. Follow the same procedure for the remaining fillets.

5. In a smaller baking dish, combine the bell peppers with olive oil and garlic powder.

6. Place the fillets and vegetables in the oven and bake for 25-30 minutes.

7. Once they are done, transfer the fillets on a serving dish. Place the cooked peppers beside the fillets and serve immediately.

8. This recipe yields 4 servings.

DINNER

Herbed Lamb and Romaine Wedges

Ingredients:

- 1 2-kilogram piece lamb leg

- ½ cup balsamic vinegar

- 1 tablespoon fresh rosemary

- 5 garlic cloves, minced

- 2 cups water

- Pinch of sea salt

- Romaine lettuce leaves, bottom trimmed off

Directions:

1. Preheat the oven to 300°F.

2. Place the lamb on a large baking dish. Sprinkle garlic and rosemary on top of the lamb then pour in water and balsamic vinegar.

3. Cover the lamb with aluminum foil and bake it in the oven for 2 hours.

4. After 2 hours, remove the foil from the lamb and turn up the heat to 400°F. Continue baking the lamb for another hour.

5. Remove the lamb from the oven. Transfer it to a dish and let it cool for 5-10 minutes. Once the lamb has cooled, use a fork to shred the lamb meat. Place the shredded meat in another plate then pour the meat drippings over it.

6. To serve the dish, get a Romaine lettuce leaf and spoon a tablespoon of the shredded lamb into the center of the leaf. Place the wedge on a serving plate and do the remaining ingredients.

7. This recipe yields 4 servings.

SNACK

Low-Calorie Flaxseed Crisps

Ingredients:

- ½ cup flaxseed meal

- 1 large egg

- ½ cup almond flour

- 2 teaspoons water

- 2 teaspoons coconut oil

- 2 teaspoons olive oil

- 1 teaspoon onion powder

- Pinch of sea salt

Directions:

1. Combine almond flour and flaxseed in a bowl and stir. Add in egg and mix well.

2. Pour water and olive oil into the mixture then season with salt and onion powder. Mix the ingredients until a doughy consistency forms.

3. Place the dough in between two sheets of wax paper and use a rolling pin to flatten it into cracker-like thickness. Slice the flattened dough into 20 equal portions.

4. Heat the coconut oil in a pan over medium-high flame. Fry the crisps in the pan for 3 minutes per side. Do this in 4 batches. Place the fried crisps on a wire rack to drain and cool completely.

5. This recipe yields 10 servings.

DAY 5

BREAKFAST

Fruity Breakfast Muffins

Ingredients:

- 1 cup dried apricots, minced

- 1 cup pitted dates, minced

- ½ teaspoon ground ginger

- 1 cup pumpkin puree

- ½ cup fresh orange juice

- 5 eggs, whisked

- ¾ cup coconut flour

- 3 tablespoons coconut oil, melted

- ½ teaspoon vanilla extract

- 1 teaspoon grated orange zest

- ½ teaspoon cinnamon powder

- ½ teaspoon baking soda

- Pinch of sea salt

Directions:

1. Preheat the oven to 350°F and lightly grease a muffin pan with cooking spray.

2. Place the orange juice, apricots, dates and zest in a saucepan over medium flame. Simmer the fruit mixture for 5-7 minutes with constant stirring. Turn off the flame.

3. Combine the flour, baking soda, salt, cinnamon powder and ginger powder in a bowl. Pour in the whisked eggs and mix well. Fold in the pumpkin puree into the batter and combine.

4. Add in the vanilla, coconut oil and the fruit mixture. Stir the muffin batter until well-combined.

5. Pour the batter into the muffin tins and bake for 30 minutes. Let it cool for 5 minutes before serving.

6. This recipe yields 10-12 servings.

LUNCH

Cold Cucumber and Celery Soup

Ingredients:

- 1 large cucumber, chopped

- 1 cup chopped celery

- 1 teaspoon minced garlic

- 2 tablespoons chopped fresh parsley

- 1 ½ cups homemade chicken broth

- 1 cup coconut milk

- ½ tablespoon lemon juice

- Pinch of salt and ground black pepper

Directions:

1. Combine cucumber, celery, chicken broth, coconut milk, lemon juice and garlic in a food processor. Process for 10 seconds or until the soup is smooth and creamy. Season the soup with salt and ground pepper.

2. Transfer the soup to an airtight container and chill in the fridge for 2 hours. Sprinkle parsley on top before serving. Serve cold.

3. This recipe yields 4 servings.

4.

DINNER

Creamy Beef Stroganoff

Ingredients:

- 500 grams beef strips

- 1 sweet onion, chopped

- ½ cup button mushrooms, sliced

- 1 cup homemade chicken stock

- ½ cup ghee

- 2 tablespoons coconut flour

- 1 tablespoon lemon juice

- ½ cup coconut cream

- Dash of sea salt and ground black pepper

Directions:

1. Heat the ghee in a skillet over medium-high flame. Arrange the beef strips on the pan then season it with salt and pepper. Sear the beef strips until the sides turn brown.

2. Add the chopped onions in the pan and sauté for 5 minutes. Remove the beef and onions from the pan, transfer them to a dish and set aside.

3. Pour the chicken stock into the pan then lower the heat to medium. Stir until the stock begins to boil. Add in the lemon juice, beef and onions. Cover the pan and simmer for 30 minutes or until the beef is tender.

4. Once the beef is tender, pour in the coconut cream and mushrooms. Continue cooking for 8-10 minutes then turn off the heat. Serve hot.

5. This recipe yields 4 servings.

SNACK

Honey and Spice Chickpeas

Ingredients:

- 4 cups chickpeas, drained

- 1 tablespoon raw honey

- 2 teaspoons paprika

- 1 teaspoon chili powder

- 1 teaspoon ground coriander

- 1 teaspoon ground cumin

- 1 teaspoon ground black pepper

- 2 teaspoons olive oil

Directions:

1. Preheat the oven to 350°F and grease a baking sheet with cooking spray.

2. Place paprika, chili powder, coriander, cumin, black pepper and olive oil in a pan over medium flame. Heat the spices for 2 minutes then turn off the stove.

3. Combine the chickpeas and heated spice mixture in a bowl then toss them together. Place the spice-coated chickpeas on the baking sheet and roast it in the oven for 1 hour.

4. Once the chickpeas are roasted, remove them from the oven and let cool for 5 minutes. Drizzle the honey over the chickpeas and let it stand for 10 minutes.

5. Transfer the chickpeas in an airtight container. Serve immediately.

6. This recipe yields 6 servings.

DAY 6

BREAKFAST

Nutty Banana Hotcakes

Ingredients:

- 4 eggs, whisked

- 3 bananas, peeled and chopped

- 4 dates, pitted and minced

- ½ cup crushed raw almonds

- ½ teaspoon cinnamon powder

- ½ teaspoon almond extract

- Dash of sea salt

- Olive oil for frying

Directions:

1. Mash the bananas in a bowl. Add in eggs, dates, almonds, cinnamon powder, almond extract and sea salt. Mix well.

2. Heat some olive oil in a pan over medium-high flame. Pour in a heaping tablespoon of the hotcake mixture into the pan and cook each side for 3 minutes. Serve warm.

3. This recipe yields 12 servings.

LUNCH

Low-Carb Cheesy Tuna Salad

Ingredients:

- 3 cups canned tuna in water, drained

- 1 cup organic mayonnaise

- 3 tablespoons fresh lime juice

- 2 tablespoons cottage cheese

- 1 cup chopped celery

- 1 cup diced cucumbers

- 2 tablespoons chopped green onions

- 2 tablespoons olive oil

- Dash of sea salt and ground black pepper

Directions:

1. Spoon the drained tuna into a salad bowl. Add in celery, cucumbers, mayonnaise, cottage cheese, lime juice and olive oil. Season the salad with salt and pepper then sprinkle green onions on top.

2. Place the tuna salad in the fridge and chill for 1-2 hours before serving.

3. This recipe yields 4 servings.

DINNER

Tangy Rosemary Chicken with Carrots

Ingredients:

- 1 medium whole chicken, cleaned

- 1 cup olive oil

- 1 tablespoon fresh rosemary

- 1 tablespoon lemon pepper seasoning

- 2 cups baby carrots

- Pinch of sea salt

Directions:

1. Preheat the oven to 300°F and lightly grease a baking dish with olive oil.

2. Position the chicken at the center of the baking dish. Pour the olive oil inside and outside the bird then rub. Season the outer part of the chicken with sea salt, lemon pepper seasoning and fresh rosemary.

3. Arrange the baby carrots at the side of the chicken.

4. Roast the chicken and carrots in the oven for 30 minutes then lower the temperature to 200°F. Continue roasting another 30 minutes or until the meat and carrots are tender.

5. Remove the pan from the oven and transfer the baby carrots on a serving dish. Baste the chicken with the juices in the pan then cover it with aluminum foil. Let the chicken sit at room temperature for 10 minutes.

6. Slice the chicken and place it on the dish with the baby carrots. Serve immediately.

7. This recipe yields 5 servings.

SNACK

Maple Fudge Bites

Ingredients:

- 2 tablespoons maple syrup

- 5 tablespoons almond butter

- 2 tablespoons coconut oil, melted

- ½ teaspoon almond extract

- ¼ teaspoon sea salt

Directions:

1. Combine maple syrup, almond butter, coconut oil, almond extract and sea salt in a heat-proof bowl. Stir then place it in the microwave. Heat the fudge mixture for 5 minutes.

2. After 5 minutes, remove the mixture from the microwave and stir until the ingredients meld together. Pour the fudge mixture into a chocolate mold tray and freeze for 2 hours.

3. This recipe yields 10 servings.

DAY 7

BREAKFAST

Savory Mushroom and Tomato Frittata

Ingredients:

- 3 eggs, whisked

- 1 cup button mushrooms, sliced thinly

- 1 medium tomato, deseeded and diced

- 1 small onion, minced

- 2 tablespoons chopped fresh parsley

- 2 garlic cloves, crushed

- Pinch of sea salt and pepper

- 2 tablespoons olive oil

Directions:

1. Heat a tablespoon of olive oil in a pan over medium-high flame. Cook the onions in the pan for 2 minutes. Add in mushrooms and garlic and sauté for another 2 minutes.

2. Pour eggs and remaining olive oil into the pan and stir. Add parsley, salt and pepper then whisk for 20 seconds.

3. Cover the pan and lower the flame to medium. Let the frittata cook for 5 minutes or until the eggs are cooked. Turn off the heat and transfer the dish to a serving plate.

4. Slice the frittata and serve immediately.

5. This recipe yields 2 servings.

LUNCH

Carrot Ginger Soup

Ingredients:

- 4 carrots, peeled and chopped

- 3 cups water

- 1 tablespoon minced garlic

- 1 tablespoon minced ginger

- ½ teaspoon turmeric powder

- 1 cup coconut cream

- 1 ½ teaspoons lemon juice

- 1 tablespoon raw honey

- Pinch of sea salt

Directions:

1. Place the chopped carrots, garlic and ginger in a saucepan then pour in water. Season the mixture with salt, turmeric powder and honey then stir.

2. Set the stove to medium-high and allow the soup to simmer for 30 minutes or until the carrots are tender. Turn off the heat.

3. Place an immersion blender in the saucepan and mix the soup until creamy. Pour coconut cream and lemon juice into the soup then stir.

4. Let the soup cool completely before placing it in the fridge. This soup is best served cold.

5. This recipe yields 3 servings.

DINNER

Chicken Adobo with Coconut Cream

Ingredients:

- 3 skinless chicken thighs, halved
- 2 skinless chicken breasts, halved
- 2 tablespoons chopped garlic
- 1 tablespoon chopped ginger
- 1 cup coconut cream
- 1 large yellow onion, minced
- 3 bay leaves
- ½ teaspoon black peppercorns
- ¾ cup coconut aminos
- ¾ cup white vinegar
- 1 tablespoon raw honey
- Dash of sea salt

Directions:

1. Arrange the chicken pieces, garlic, ginger, bay leaves and onions in a slow cooker. Mix in coconut aminos, honey and white vinegar. Finally, season the dish with peppercorns and sea salt. If you want more sauce for your adobo, pour in ½ cup of water.

2. Cover the pot then cook the dish on high temperature for 3 hours. After 3 hours, pour in the coconut cream and stir. Cover the pot and continue cooking the adobo for another hour.

3. Transfer the chicken pieces on a serving bowl then pour the coconut adobo sauce over the meat. Discard the bay leaves and serve.

4. This recipe makes yields 3-4 servings.

SNACK

Vanilla Coconut Cookies

Ingredients:

- 1 teaspoon vanilla extract

- 3 cups grated coconut

- 1 banana, peeled and mashed

- ½ cup raw honey

- Dash of sea salt

Directions:

1. Preheat the oven to 350°F and line a cookie sheet with parchment paper.

2. Place the coconut, banana, honey, vanilla and salt in a food processor. Blend until the ingredients are well-combined.

3. Form 12 balls from the cookie mixture and gradually flatten them on the palm of your hand. Arrange the cookies on the cookie sheet. Bake for 12-15 minutes in the oven.

4. Let the cookies cool for 10 minutes before serving.

Chapter 5: Week 2 Recipes

DAY 8

BREAKFAST

High-Fiber Pineapple Smoothie

Ingredients:

- 2 cups fresh pineapple chunks

- 3 tablespoons flaxseed meal

- 2 cups coconut milk

- 1 cup water

- 2 tablespoons raw honey

- 3 tablespoons nut butter

Directions:

1. Place the pineapple chunks in a blender. Add in flaxseed, milk, water, nut butter, and honey. Process the drink until smooth and creamy.

2. Pour into individual glasses and serve immediately.

3. This recipe yields 4 servings.

LUNCH

Chicken Avocado Burgers

Ingredients:

- 400 grams ground chicken meat

- ½ cup mashed avocado

- ½ cup finely-chopped celery

- 1 large egg, whisked

- 1 sweet onion, minced

- 1 teaspoon garlic powder

- ¼ cup grated Parmesan cheese

- 1 tablespoon almond flour

- 2 tablespoons olive oil

- Dash of sea salt and ground black pepper

Directions:

1. Place the ground chicken in a bowl then add in egg, avocado, Parmesan, almond flour, celery and onions. Season the mixture with garlic powder, salt and pepper then mix well.

2. Use your hands to form 6 patties from the mixture. Place the patties on a plate and chill them in the fridge for 30 minutes.

3. Heat the olive oil in a pan over medium-high flame. Once the oil is hot, place the burger patties on the pan and cook for 8 minutes. Flip the burgers and cook the remaining side for 5 minutes or until golden brown.

4. Let the burgers cool for 5 minutes then serve.

5. This recipe yields 6 servings.

DINNER

Italian-style Braised Mussels

Ingredients:

- 35 fresh mussels, cleaned and beards discarded
- 4 large tomatoes, diced
- 1 tablespoon minced ginger
- 2 tablespoons minced garlic
- 2 tablespoons chopped fresh parsley
- 1 tablespoon ghee
- ½ cup white wine
- 1 cup water
- 1 tablespoon olive oil
- ½ teaspoon sea salt

Directions:

1. Soak the mussels in cold water for 30 minutes. Completely drain the water from the mussels and set aside.

2. Heat the olive oil in a soup pot over medium flame. Add the garlic and sauté for 1 minute. Pour in the tomatoes and continue cooking for 4 minutes.

3. Slowly add in the water, ghee, wine and ginger. Cover the pot and let the mixture simmer for 10 minutes.

4. Open the cover and pour in the mussels. Season with sea salt and sprinkle parsley on top. Cover the pot then simmer the mussels for another 10 minutes. Once the mussels have opened, they are ready to serve.

5. This recipe yields 4 servings.

SNACK

No-Cook Date Bars

Ingredients:

- 1 cup sesame seeds

- ½ cup ground walnuts

- ½ cup ground almonds

- 3 cups pitted dates, chopped

- Pinch of sea salt

Directions:

1. Place the dates, sesame seeds, walnuts, almonds and salt in a food processor and mix well. Add a few drops of water if you want to moisten the mixture.

2. Pour the mixture in a rectangular baking pan, making sure to spread it evenly towards the sides. Place it in the fridge and chill for 2 hours.

3. Slice the date mixture into 24 portions then transfer them into an airtight container.

4. This recipe yields 12 servings.

DAY 9

BREAKFAST

Crockpot Brown Rice Cereal

Ingredients:

- 3 cups water

- 3 cups coconut milk

- 1 cup medium grain brown rice

- 2 teaspoons cinnamon powder

- ½ cup lemon juice

- ½ teaspoon sea salt

- 8 dates, pitted and minced

Directions:

1. Pour the brown rice into a small crockpot. Add in the dates, salt and cinnamon powder then stir. Pour in water, coconut milk and lemon juice.

2. Cover the pot and cook the cereal for 5-6 hours on low temperature. You may add more water if the sauce is too thick. Pour into smaller bowls and serve hot.

3. This recipe yields 4 servings.

LUNCH

Cold String Bean Salad

Ingredients:

- 500 grams string beans, chopped into 1 ½ inch slices

- 2 tablespoons olive oil

- 2 tablespoons fresh lemon juice

- 1 tablespoon Dijon mustard

- 1 teaspoon raw honey

- 2 teaspoons homemade chicken broth

- 1 tablespoon minced sweet onions

- Pinch of sea salt and ground black pepper

Directions:

1. Boil the string beans in water for 4 minutes. Once the string beans are tender, remove them from the pot then transfer them immediately to a bowl of ice water. After 2 minutes, drain the water completely. Place the string beans in a salad bowl and set aside.

2. Whisk together lemon juice, olive oil, mustard, honey, chicken broth, sweet onions, sea salt and pepper.

3. Pour the dressing into the bowl of string beans then toss the salad. Chill the salad in the fridge for 2 hours then serve.

4. This recipe yields 4 servings.

DINNER

Crockpot Chicken Stew

Ingredients:

- 3 large chicken breasts, chopped into serving portions

- 1 cup pureed tomatoes

- ½ cup homemade chicken stock

- 1 tablespoon minced garlic

- ½ teaspoon chili powder

- ¼ cup minced onion

- 1 tablespoon minced ginger

- 1 tablespoon maple syrup

- 2 tablespoons coconut aminos

- 1 small chili pepper, deseeded and chopped

- ½ cup crushed pineapple

- 1 tablespoon olive oil

Directions:

1. Combine tomato puree, crushed pineapple, olive oil, garlic, onion, ginger, chili powder, maple syrup and coconut aminos in a medium crockpot and stir. Pour chicken broth into the pot and mix well.

2. One at a time, place the chicken pieces into the pot then sprinkle chopped chili peppers on top. Cover the crockpot and cook the stew on high for 4 hours.

3. Remove the chicken pieces from the pot and transfer to a serving bowl. Pour the sauce over the meat and serve immediately.

4. This recipe yields 6 servings.

SNACK

Choco-Coated Banana Lollipops

Ingredients:

- 3 large bananas, peeled and sliced into three

- 2 tablespoons grated coconut

- 2 tablespoons crushed cashews

- 1 cup dark chocolate chips

- 1 tablespoon coconut oil

Directions:

1. Place the chocolate chips and coconut oil in a heat-proof bowl and microwave for 20 seconds. Stir the melted chocolate chips and microwave again for 20-30 more seconds until the chocolate is smooth and runny.

2. Skewer each banana piece with a popsicle stick. Dip the banana into the chocolate then sprinkle cashews and coconut around the fruit. Do the same procedure for the rest of the bananas.

3. Place the banana snacks in the freezer for 2-3 hours. This snack is best served chilled.

4. This recipe yields 9 servings.

DAY 10

BREAKFAST

Sunrise Fruit Shake

Ingredients:

- 6 mint leaves

- 2 cups freshly-chopped mango

- 2 oranges, peeled and sectioned

- 1 cup fresh raspberries

- 1 cup coconut milk

- ½ cup water

Directions:

1. Place the mangoes, oranges, raspberries and mint leaves in a blender and pulse. Pour in coconut milk and water.

2. Blend the ingredients for 30-40 seconds then pour into glasses. Serve immediately.

3. This recipe yields 2 servings.

LUNCH

Pork Chops with Lime Coconut Gravy

Ingredients:

- 3 medium pork chops

- 200 grams fresh cremini mushrooms, chopped

- 1 ½ cups coconut cream

- 2 teaspoons lime juice

- 1 white onion, minced

- 2 teaspoons minced garlic

- ½ cup homemade chicken stock

- 1 tablespoon olive oil

- Pinch of sea salt and ground black pepper

Directions:

1. Season the pork chops with salt, pepper and minced garlic. Set aside.

2. Heat the olive oil in a pan over medium-high flame. Place the chops on the pan and cook for 6 minutes. Flip them over then cook the remaining side for 4-5 minutes.

3. Once the chops have been seared, add the chicken stock, coconut cream and onions to the pan. Cover the pan and simmer the dish for 20 minutes. Pour in the lime juice then cook for another 5 minutes.

4. Once the pork chops are tender, adjust the heat to medium-low then transfer the pork chops into a serving dish.

5. Simmer the sauce for another 2 minutes while stirring it together with the meat drippings on the pan. Pour the gravy on top of the pork chops. Serve immediately.

6. This recipe yields 3 servings.

DINNER

Cream of Broccoli and Chicken Soup

Ingredients:

- 3 cups broccoli florets

- 2 cups chopped zucchini

- 1 sweet onion, minced

- 1 tablespoon olive oil

- 2 ½ cups homemade chicken stock

- ½ cup coconut cream

- 1 small cooked chicken breast, finely chopped

- 3 green onions, chopped

- Pinch of sea salt and ground black pepper

Directions:

1. Heat the oil in a saucepan over medium-high flame. Once the oil is hot, add in the broccoli and zucchini and cook for 10 minutes. Transfer the vegetables to a bowl and set aside.

2. In the same saucepan, sauté the onions and chopped chicken breasts for 5 minutes or until the onions are translucent. Add in the broccoli and zucchini and continue cooking for 5 more minutes.

3. Pour the chicken stock into the saucepan, cover the pot and let the mixture simmer for 10 minutes.

4. After 10 minutes, lower the flame then add in the coconut cream. Continue cooking for 2-3 minutes then turn off the heat.

5. Pour the soup into a blender then process for 10 seconds. Once the soup is creamy, pour this into individual bowls and top with green onions. Serve immediately.

6. This recipe yields 4 servings.

SNACK

Homemade Spicy Kale Chips

Ingredients:

- 500 grams kale leaves, washed and drained

- 2 teaspoons sea salt

- 1 tablespoon garlic powder

- 2 teaspoons cayenne pepper

- 1 tablespoon olive oil

Directions:

1. Preheat the oven to 350°F and line a baking sheet with parchment paper.

2. In a bowl, combine torn kale leaves, olive oil, cayenne pepper, garlic powder and sea salt. Toss the ingredients until all the leaves are evenly coated.

3. Arrange the vegetables on the baking sheet. Place it in the oven and bake for 15 minutes. Transfer the kale chips on a wire rack and let it cool for 10 minutes before serving.

4. This recipe yields 8 servings.

BREAKFAST

Baked Mediterranean Quiche

Ingredients:

- 1 cup sun-dried tomatoes, chopped

- 1 cup freshly-chopped parsley

- 1 cup black olives, pitted and sliced

- ½ cup cottage cheese

- 8 eggs, whisked

- Dash of sea salt

Directions:

1. Preheat the oven to 350°F and grease a round baking dish with olive oil.

2. Pour the eggs into a bowl then add in the tomatoes, olives, cottage cheese and parsley. Season with sea salt then whisk the ingredients together.

3. Pour the quiche mixture into the baking dish. Bake it in the oven for 25-30 minutes. Let the quiche cool for 5 minutes then slice into 6 equal portions.

4. This recipe yields 6 servings.

LUNCH

High-Fiber Mixed Greens Soup

Ingredients:

- 1 bunch kale leaves, trimmed and washed

- ½ cup spinach leaves

- ½ head small cabbage, shredded

- 1 cup shredded lettuce

- 2 teaspoons chopped green onions

- 2 cups homemade chicken stock

- 2 cups water

- Pinch of thyme

- Pinch of sea salt

Directions:

1. Combine kale, cabbage, lettuce, spinach and green onions in a blender and pulse until the leaves are finely chopped. Transfer the chopped greens into a slow cooker.

2. Add chicken stock, water, thyme and sea salt into the slow cooker then stir the ingredients together. Cover the pot and cook the soup on high for 4 hours.

3. This recipe yields 4 servings.

DINNER

Stir-Fried Spicy Asian Chicken

Ingredients:

- 3 large chicken breasts, skinned and deboned

- 3 tablespoons raw honey

- 1 tablespoon sesame oil

- 2 tablespoons coconut aminos

- 1 tablespoon tomato paste

- 1 tablespoon chili powder

- 1 tablespoon minced ginger

- 3 tablespoons water

- 1 tablespoon olive oil

- Pinch of sea salt

Directions:

1. Combine honey, sesame oil, coconut aminos, tomato paste and chili powder in a bowl and whisk them together. Set aside.

2. Cut the chicken breasts into small chunks. Season it with salt.

3. Heat the oil in a pan over medium-high flame. Cook the chicken chunks for 6-7 minutes or until light brown. Add in the ginger and stir-fry for 1 minute.

4. Pour the honey sesame mixture into the pan and stir-fry for 1 minute. Add water and cover the pan. Let it simmer for 2 minutes then stir.

5. Transfer the dish to a serving plate and serve immediately.

6. This recipe yields 6 servings.

SNACK

Fruit and Nut Snack Mix

Ingredients:

- ½ cup slivered almonds

- ½ cup chopped walnuts

- ½ cup chopped hazelnuts

- 1 cup sunflower seeds

- ½ cup dried cherries, diced

- ½ cup dried apricots, minced

- ½ cup dates, pitted and chopped

- 1 cup golden raisins

Directions:

1. Place the almonds, walnuts, hazelnuts, sunflower seeds, cherries, apricots, dates and raisins in a bowl and toss them together. Place them in individual sandwich bags and store.

2. This recipe yields 10 servings.

DAY 12

BREAKFAST

Poached Egg with Sautéed Collards

Ingredients:

- 2 large eggs
- 2 cups chopped collard greens
- ½ cup chopped leeks
- 2 cups water
- ½ teaspoon apple cider vinegar
- 3 garlic cloves, minced
- 1 tablespoon fresh lime juice
- 3 tablespoons homemade chicken stock
- Pinch of sea salt and ground black pepper

Directions:

1. Heat the chicken stock in a pan over medium high flame. Add in garlic and leeks then cook for 2 minutes.

2. Add collard greens, lime juice, salt and pepper into the pan and cover it. Lower the flame and let the greens simmer for 5 minutes. Once the greens are cooked, transfer it to a serving platter and set aside.

3. Heat the water and vinegar in a saucepan over medium-high flame. Once the water starts to simmer, crack the eggs one at a time into the vinegar water. Let the egg poach for 4-5 minutes.

4. Remove the egg from the vinegar water by using a slotted spoon. Place the eggs on the sautéed greens and serve immediately.

5. This recipe yields 2 servings.

LUNCH

Shrimp and Zucchini Pasta

Ingredients:

- 1 large zucchini

- 1 cup frozen shrimp, thawed

- 2 tablespoons chicken stock

- 10 cherry tomatoes, halved

- 1 teaspoon minced garlic

- 1 tablespoon olive oil

- 2 tablespoons grated Parmesan cheese

- ½ cup fresh basil

- 2 tablespoons lemon juice

- Pinch of sea salt

- Pinch of cayenne pepper

Directions:

1. Heat the oil in a pan over medium high flame. Add the garlic, tomatoes and shrimp and sauté for 5 minutes.

2. While the shrimp is cooking, use a spiralizer to cut the zucchini into long noodles. Trim the noodles and set aside.

3. Once the shrimps are ready, add lemon juice and chicken stock. Mix in the zucchini noodles then season with salt and cayenne pepper. Stir the dish while cooking for 5 minutes.

4. Turn off the heat then mix in the fresh basil. Transfer the pasta dish to a serving bowl and top with grated Parmesan cheese. Serve immediately.

5. This recipe yields 2 servings.

DINNER

Fiery Tomato and Cabbage Soup

Ingredients:

- 3 cups diced tomatoes

- 1 cup shredded cabbage

- 1 ½ cups coconut cream

- 1 tablespoon olive oil

- 1 ½ cups homemade chicken stock

- 1 sweet onion, minced

- 1 teaspoon coconut flour

- 1 teaspoon chili powder

- ½ teaspoon red pepper flakes

- Pinch of sea salt and ground black pepper

Directions:

1. Heat the oil in a pot over medium-high flame. Add the onions and red pepper flakes and cook for 5 minutes.

2. Mix in tomatoes, cabbage, coconut flour and chicken stock. Lower the flame to medium then cover the pot. Let the soup simmer for 1 hour.

3. After 1 hour, pour in the coconut cream then season with sea salt and pepper. Stir the soup then turn off the flame. Serve while hot.

4. This recipe yields 6 servings.

SNACK

Pepper, Tomato, and Cheese Salad

Ingredients:

- ½ cup chopped yellow bell pepper

- ½ cup chopped green bell pepper

- 1 ½ cups cottage cheese

- 1 cup chopped tomato

- 1 teaspoon lemon juice

- 1 tablespoon chopped parsley

- Pinch of salt and ground black pepper

Directions:

1. Mix together the bell peppers, lemon juice, tomato and parsley. Season the vegetables with salt and pepper.

2. Transfer the salad to a serving platter and pour the cottage cheese on top of the veggies. Serve immediately or chill it in the fridge for 1-2 hours.

3. This recipe yields 3 servings.

DAY 13

BREAKFAST

Mini Breakfast Banana Loaves

Ingredients:

- 350 grams chopped bananas

- 1 ½ cup chopped walnuts

- 1 ½ cup desiccated coconut

- ½ teaspoon cinnamon powder

- 1 tablespoon maple syrup

- Drop of vanilla extract

- Dash of sea salt

Directions:

1. Preheat the oven to 350°F and line a cake pan with parchment paper.

2. Pour the bananas, walnuts, maple syrup, coconut, cinnamon powder, vanilla and salt into a food processor. Mix until a creamy batter is formed.

3. Gradually pour the batter into the cake pan and spread the mixture evenly. Bake for 30 minutes then let it cool for 10 minutes. Slice and serve immediately.

4. This recipe yields 6 servings.

LUNCH

Sliced Pork with Applesauce

Ingredients:

- 1 3-lb pork shoulder cut in half

- 1 cup coconut sugar

- 2 tablespoons coconut flour

- 2 tablespoons water

- 2 apples, peeled, cored and pureed

- 2 tablespoons coconut aminos

- 1 teaspoon minced garlic

- 1 teaspoon minced ginger

- ½ teaspoon sea salt

- ½ teaspoon ground black pepper

- Pinch of cinnamon powder

Directions:

1. Rub the coconut sugar, salt and ground black pepper all over the pork shoulder. Place the pork in a crockpot.

2. Pour the pureed apples and coconut aminos on the pork. Cover the pot and cook the meat on low for 6 hours.

3. After 6 hours, remove the pork from the crockpot and let it cool on a chopping board.

4. Pour the liquids from the pot into a saucepan. Add in garlic, ginger, water and coconut flour. Whisk the ingredients then let it simmer on medium heat for 15 minutes.

5. Slice the pork shoulder into thin wedges. Pour the sauce over the meat then serve immediately.

6. This recipe yields 6 servings.

DINNER

Tomato, Avocado, and Cucumber Salad

Ingredients:

- 2 cups cherry tomatoes, halved
- 1 large cucumber, peeled and chopped
- 1 cup diced avocado
- 1 sweet onion, chopped
- ¼ cup chopped fresh parsley
- 4 tablespoons olive oil
- 3 tablespoons lemon juice
- 1 teaspoon raw honey
- Pinch of sea salt and ground black pepper

Directions:

1. Whisk together olive oil, lemon juice, honey, sea salt and pepper. Pour the dressing into a salad bowl.

2. Add the tomatoes, avocados, cucumbers, onions and parsley into the salad bowl then toss the vegetables with the dressing.

3. Chill the salad in the fridge for 1 hour. Serve immediately.

4. This recipe makes 4 servings.

SNACK

Fruit and Cheese Sticks

Ingredients:

- 12 seedless grapes

- 12 fresh kiwi chunks

- 6 dried apricots

- 12 organic Cheddar cheese cubes

Directions:

1. Soak 12 wooden skewers in water for 1 hour then drain.

2. Use a skewer to make a kebab, using this order: grape, cheese, kiwi, apricot, kiwi, cheese and grape. Follow the same procedure for the rest of the ingredients until you have 6 sticks.

3. Chill the sticks in the fridge for 1 hour. This snack is best served cold.

4. This recipe yields 6 servings.

DAY 14

BREAKFAST

Sweet Potato and Sorghum Porridge

Ingredients:

- 1 large sweet potato, boiled and peeled

- 1 cup sorghum

- 2 tablespoons raw honey

- 1 cup almond milk

- 2 cups water

- Drop of vanilla extract

Directions:

1. Mash the sweet potato in a bowl then spoon it into a slow cooker. Add in sorghum, honey, almond milk, water and vanilla extract. Mix well.

2. Cover the pot and set the temperature to low. Cook the porridge for 7 hours then turn off the heat. Mix well then let it cool completely.

3. Place the cooled porridge in the fridge for 2 hours. This dish is best served cold with an extra dash of almond milk.

4. This recipe yields 4 servings.

LUNCH

Quick-Braised Scallops

Ingredients:

- 250 grams large sea scallops

- 1 tablespoon lemon juice

- 1 tablespoon sesame oil

- 1 tablespoon homemade chicken stock

- 2 garlic cloves, chopped

- Pinch of sea salt and ground black pepper

Directions:

1. Heat the stock in a pan over medium flame. Place the chopped garlic and scallops in the pan and cook for 3 minutes. Flip the scallops over then cook the remaining side for 2 minutes.

2. Quickly transfer the scallops from the pan to a serving dish. Top the scallops with the garlic, sesame oil, lemon juice, salt and pepper. Serve immediately.

3. This recipe yields 2 servings.

DINNER

Baked Pork Tenderloin

Ingredients:

- 900 grams pork tenderloin, sliced into 3

- 3 tablespoons maple syrup

- 3 tablespoons finely chopped almonds

- ¾ cup coconut aminos

- 1 tablespoon minced garlic

- 1 tablespoon minced ginger

- 1 tablespoon olive oil

Directions:

1. Mix together the maple syrup, coconut aminos, garlic, ginger and olive oil in a large bowl. Place the tenderloin in the same bowl and let it marinade in the fridge overnight.

2. Preheat the oven to 375°F.

3. Take out the marinated tenderloin from the fridge. Dredge the pork into the chopped almonds, making sure that the sides are evenly-coated.

4. Place the meat on a baking dish. Bake the tenderloin for 30 minutes or until the pork is tender.

5. Slice the tenderloin and serve immediately.

SNACK

Crusted Zucchini Chips

Ingredients:

- 1 large zucchini, sliced thinly

- 2 egg whites, whisked

- ¾ cup ground flaxseed

- ½ teaspoon ground black pepper

- 2 tablespoons Parmesan cheese

- 1 teaspoon olive oil

Directions:

1. Preheat the oven to 250°F and lightly grease a baking sheet with olive oil.

2. Combine flaxseed, pepper and Parmesan cheese in a bowl and toss them together.

3. Dip each zucchini slice in the egg whites then dredge them in the flaxseed mixture. Arrange the coated vegetables on the baking sheet.

4. Bake the zucchini slices for 5 minutes, flip it over then bake for another 5-7 minutes. Serve immediately.

5. This recipe yields 4 servings.

Chapter 6: Week 3 Recipes

DAY 15

BREAKFAST

Mighty Green Smoothie

Ingredients:

- 2 green apples, peeled, cored and halved

- 3 cucumbers, peeled and chopped

- 1 cup fresh lemon juice

- 2 cups chopped fresh parsley

- 2 celery stalks, chopped

- 1 tablespoon minced ginger

- 1 teaspoon raw honey

Directions:

1. Place green apples, cucumbers and celery stalks in a food processor and blend for 10 seconds. Add in the parsley, ginger, honey and lemon juice. Process the ingredients for 30 seconds.

2. Pour the smoothie into glasses and serve immediately.

3. This recipe yields 3-4 servings.

LUNCH

Pan-Fried Salmon with Yoghurt Sauce

Ingredients:

- 2 medium salmon fillets

- ¼ teaspoon sea salt

- Pinch of ground black pepper

- 1 tablespoon olive oil

- 2 teaspoons lime juice

- ½ cup plain organic yoghurt

- 2 mint leaves, minced

- Pinch of ground black pepper

- ½ cup minced cucumber

Directions:

1. Rub salt, pepper and lime juice on all sides of the salmon. Let it stand for 3 minutes.

2. Heat the oil in a pan over medium high flame. Place the salmon on the pan, skin-side down. Cook the fillets for 4 minutes. Flip the fillets over and cook the remaining side for 3 minutes.

3. Transfer the salmon fillets to a serving dish.

4. To make the sauce, whisk together yoghurt, cucumbers, pepper and mint leaves. Pour the sauce over the salmon and serve immediately.

5. This recipe yields 2 servings.

DINNER

Beef and Cauliflower Rice Bowl

Ingredients:

- 600 grams ground beef

- 3 cups water

- 1 large cauliflower head, sliced into chunks

- 1 red bell pepper, deseeded and julienned

- 1 cup chopped green onions

- 1 tablespoon minced garlic

- 1 small onion, chopped

- 1 tablespoon coconut aminos

- 1 tablespoon olive oil

Directions:

1. To make the cauliflower rice, place the cauliflower chunks and water in a blender. Mix until a rice-like consistency forms. Pour the cauliflower mixture through a colander to drain the water completely. Set aside.

2. Heat the oil in a skillet over high flame. Add in the onions and garlic and cook until the onions are translucent.

3. Place the beef into the skillet and stir with the onions and garlic. Cover the pot and let it cook for 15-20 minutes.

4. Once the beef is cooked, add in the bell peppers and green onions. Continue cooking for 5 minutes.

5. Pour in the cauliflower rice into the beef and stir-fry the ingredients together. Let the dish cook for 5 minutes with constant stirring.

6. Turn off the flame then transfer the dish to individual bowls. Serve immediately.

SNACK

Whole Wheat Onion Crackers

Ingredients:

- 3 ½ cups whole wheat flour

- 1 cup chopped green onions

- ½ cup olive oil

- 1 cup water

- 1 teaspoon garlic powder

- 2 teaspoons sea salt

Directions:

1. Preheat the oven to 350 °F and prepare a baking sheet.

2. Combine whole wheat flour, green onions, garlic powder and a teaspoon of salt in a bowl. Add in water and olive oil then mix well.

3. Sprinkle flour on a large, flat surface then place the dough in the middle. Use a rolling pin to flatten the dough.

4. Transfer the dough on the baking sheet, score the dough into squares and sprinkle the remaining salt all over it. Bake for 20 minutes or until crisp and brown.

5. This recipe yields 20 servings.

DAY 16

BREAKFAST

Thyme Turkey Patties

Ingredients:

- 550 grams ground turkey meat

- 2 tablespoons fresh thyme

- 3 tablespoons almond flour

- 3 tablespoons coconut flour

- 1 large egg, whisked

- 1 tablespoon minced garlic

- 1 tablespoon raw honey

- Pinch of sea salt and ground black pepper

- Olive oil for frying

Directions:

1. Combine turkey meat, thyme, almond flour, egg, garlic, honey, salt and pepper in a bowl. Use your hands to knead the patty mixture.

2. Create 8 turkey patties from the mixture and dredge each one into the coconut flour. Set aside.

3. Heat the olive oil in a pan over medium-high flame. Cook the patties for 6 minutes or until golden brown. Flip them over and cook the remaining side for 5 minutes. Let the patties cool for 5 minutes before serving.

4. This recipe yields 4 servings.

LUNCH

Hearty Tomato and Seafood Soup

Ingredients:

- 400 grams black cod fillets, cut into chunks

- 200 grams squid rings

- 1 cup pureed tomatoes

- 1 cup chopped celery

- 2 teaspoons olive oil

- 1 cup homemade chicken stock

- ¼ teaspoon chili pepper

- 1 tablespoon chopped garlic

- 1 tablespoon chopped fresh parsley

Directions:

1. Heat the oil in a saucepan over medium-high flame. Place the garlic, chili pepper and celery in the pan then sauté for 5 minutes.

2. Pour in pureed tomatoes and chicken stock then cover the pot. Simmer the soup for 10 minutes.

3. After 10 minutes, place the cod fillets and squid rings into the pot and stir. Let the soup simmer for 5 minutes or until the cod becomes flaky when poked by a fork.

4. Turn off the flame then transfer the soup to individual bowls. Sprinkle parsley on top then serve immediately.

5. This recipe yields 3 servings.

DINNER

Grilled Chicken with Green Herb Sauce

Ingredients:

- 4 small chicken breast halves, boneless and skinless

- ½ teaspoon sea salt

- ½ teaspoon ground black pepper

- 3 tablespoons olive oil

- 2 tablespoons red wine vinegar

- ½ cup chopped fresh parsley

- ½ teaspoon dried oregano

- 1 tablespoon minced garlic

- 3 mint leaves

- ¼ teaspoon red pepper flakes

Directions:

1. To make the herb sauce, place 2 tablespoons olive oil, red wine vinegar, parsley, oregano, garlic, mint leaves and pepper flakes in a food processor. Process the ingredients until the herbs are finely-chopped. Pour the sauce into a small bowl and set aside.

2. Place the chicken breasts in between two sheets of wax paper and use a rolling pin to slightly flatten the meat. Rub salt, pepper and the remaining olive oil on all sides of the chicken breasts. Place them on a grill pan over medium-high flame.

3. Grill each side for 5 minutes. Let the chicken sit at room temperature for 5 minutes then slice each breast into 4 pieces.

4. Arrange the chicken slices on a dish. Place the herb sauce on the side and serve immediately.

5. This recipe yields 4 servings.

SNACK

Creamy Mango Coolers

Ingredients:

- 2 cups pureed ripe mangoes

- 1 cup coconut milk

- 2 tablespoons raw honey

- ½ teaspoon chia seeds

Directions:

1. Process the mango puree, coconut milk, honey and chia seeds in a blender until smooth and creamy.

2. Pour the mixture into 8 popsicle molds and freeze for 8 hours. Serve these snacks straight from the freezer.

3. This recipe yields 8 servings.

DAY 17

BREAKFAST

Quinoa, Scallions, and Cheese Waffles

Ingredients:

- 1 cup quinoa flour

- 1 cup almond flour

- 2 eggs, whisked

- 4 teaspoons baking powder

- 2 tablespoons chopped scallions

- ½ cup cottage cheese

- 2 cups almond milk

- ¼ cup sesame oil

- Pinch of sea salt

Directions:

1. Combine almond flour, quinoa flour, baking powder and salt in a bowl and mix well. Set aside.

2. In another bowl, mix together eggs, cottage cheese, almond milk and sesame oil. Whisk the wet ingredients together.

3. Pour the wet ingredients into the bowl of dry ingredients and mix well. Pour the batter into a pre-heated waffle pan.

4. Cook the waffles for 6 minutes or until golden brown.

5. This recipe yields 10 servings.

LUNCH

Shrimp and Avocado Salad

Ingredients:

- 6 cups cooked shrimp

- 4 large avocados, halved and pitted

- 4 tablespoons lemon juice

- 4 tablespoons organic mayonnaise

- 2 cups shredded Romaine lettuce

- 1 tablespoon chili powder

- Dash of sea salt and ground black pepper

Directions:

1. Scoop out the meat from the avocados and place them in a bowl. Use a knife to cut small avocado cubes.

2. Place the avocado cubes, shrimp, mayonnaise, lettuce, lemon juice, chili powder, salt and pepper in a salad bowl. Toss the ingredients together and place it in the fridge for 1 hour. Serve cold.

3. This recipe yields 8 servings.

DINNER

Oven-Baked Spicy Chicken Wings

Ingredients:

- 700 grams chicken wings

- 1 teaspoon dried rosemary

- ½ teaspoon dried cumin

- 1 teaspoon dried oregano

- 1 tablespoon dried basil

- 1 tablespoon garlic powder

- 1 teaspoon sea salt

- 2 tablespoons grated Parmesan cheese

- 2 tablespoons olive oil

Directions:

1. Preheat the oven to 400°F and prepare a baking sheet lined with parchment paper.

2. Combine oregano, salt, cumin, garlic powder and rosemary in a bowl. Place the chicken wings inside the bowl of spices and toss them together.

3. Lay the chicken wings on the baking sheet, place them in the oven and bake for 30 minutes.

4. In a separate bowl, whisk together basil, olive oil and Parmesan cheese. Place the cooked wings inside and toss until the wings are well-coated. Serve immediately.

5. This recipe yields 4 servings.

SNACK

Pineapple Cucumber Smoothie

Ingredients:

- 2 cups fresh pineapple chunks

- 1 cup chopped cucumber

- 1 teaspoon powdered ginger

- 1 large banana, chopped

- 1 ½ cups coconut water

Directions:

1. Place pineapple chunks, cucumber, ginger and banana in a blender and pulse. Pour the coconut water into the blender and process for 20 seconds.

2. Serve the smoothie in individual glasses.

3. This recipe yields 2 servings.

DAY 18

BREAKFAST

Salmon Breakfast Cups

Ingredients:

- 125 grams smoked salmon, chopped

- 6 eggs, whisked

- 1 tablespoon coconut cream

- 3 tablespoons coconut milk

- 3 tablespoons cottage cheese

- 6 egg whites

- ½ small onion, minced

- 1 tablespoon olive oil

- 1 teaspoon garlic powder

- Pinch of sea salt

Directions:

1. Preheat the oven to 325°F. Lightly grease 6 ramekins with cooking spray. Set aside.

2. Heat the olive oil in a pan over medium-high flame. Cook the onions in the pan for 4 minutes then add in salmon, salt and garlic powder. Sauté for 3 minutes then turn off the flame.

3. Place even portions of the cooked salmon into the ramekins.

4. Whisk together eggs, egg whites, cottage cheese, coconut milk and coconut cream. Pour the egg mixture into each ramekin.

5. Place the ramekins in the oven and bake for 30 minutes. Let the cups cool for 10 minutes. Unmold the salmon cups let it cool for 5 minutes before serving.

6. This recipe yields 6 servings.

LUNCH

Shredded Pork and Vegetable Stew

Ingredients:

- 700 grams pork chops, deboned and fat trimmed off

- 2 tablespoons olive oil

- 2 cups chopped tomatoes

- 1 sweet onion, minced

- 1 tablespoon minced garlic

- 1 ½ cups diced sugar beets

- 1 teaspoon sea salt

- ½ teaspoon cumin

- 1 tablespoon cayenne pepper

- ½ teaspoon ground black pepper

- 4 cups homemade vegetable stock

- 4 tablespoons lemon juice

Directions:

1. Place the pork chops at the bottom of a slow cooker pot. Add in tomatoes, olive oil, onion, garlic, beets, salt, cumin, cayenne pepper and black pepper.

2. Pour the vegetable stock into the pot. Cover it then cook the stew on low temperature for 8 hours.

3. After 8 hours, take out the pork from the pot and use a fork to shred it. Place the shredded pork in a large soup bowl then pour in the soup from the slow cooker. Mix well.

4. Pour lemon juice over the soup before serving.

5. This recipe yields 7 servings.

Balsamic Jicama and Apple Salad

Ingredients:

- 2 large green apples, cored and julienned

- 1 large jicama, peeled and julienned

- ¼ cup golden raisins

- 2 tablespoons chopped shallots

- 1 tablespoon lemon juice

- 1 tablespoon balsamic vinegar

- 1 tablespoon olive oil

- Pinch of sea salt and ground black pepper

- Parmesan cheese shavings

Directions:

1. To make the dressing, whisk together lemon juice, balsamic vinegar, olive oil, sea salt and pepper.

2. Place the apples, jicamas, raisins, shallots and balsamic dressing in a bowl and toss them until well-combined.

3. Use a potato peeler to make Parmesan cheese shavings and sprinkle them on top of the tossed salad. Serve immediately.

4. This recipe yields 4 servings.

SNACK

Low-Sodium Turnip Fries

Ingredients:

- 4 turnips, peeled and sliced into thick strips

- 1 teaspoon chili powder

- 1 teaspoon onion powder

- 2 tablespoons coconut oil, melted

- Pinch of sea salt and ground black pepper

Directions:

1. Preheat the oven to 375°F and prepare a baking sheet lined with parchment paper.

2. Combine the turnips and coconut oil in a large bowl and toss them together. Season the fries with chili powder, onion

powder, sea salt and pepper then toss it again for an even coating.

3. Place the turnips on the baking sheet and bake it in the oven for 30 minutes. To check if the turnip fries are ready, poke the vegetables with a fork.

4. Let the turnip fries cool at room temperature for 10 minutes then serve.

5. This recipe yields 8 servings.

DAY 19

BREAKFAST

Green Breakfast Salad with Soft-Boiled Eggs

Ingredients:

- 2 large eggs, soft-boiled

- 4 cups arugula leaves, washed and drained

- 1 cup cherry tomatoes, halved

- 2 bacon slices, cooked and chopped

- 3 teaspoons balsamic vinegar

- 3 teaspoons olive oil

- ½ teaspoon ground black pepper

- Dash of sea salt

Directions:

1. Whisk together oil, balsamic vinegar, salt and pepper in a salad bowl. Add in the arugula leaves, cherry tomatoes and chopped bacon. Toss the salad then chill it in the fridge for 1 hour.

2. Remove the salad from the fridge. Peel the shells from the eggs and slowly slice the eggs in half. Arrange the eggs on top of the salad then serve immediately.

3. This recipe yields 2 servings.

LUNCH

Chunky Tilapia Chowder

Ingredients:

- 500 grams tilapia fillets, cut into small cubes
- 1 cup coconut cream
- 1 cup coconut milk
- 3 cups diced sweet potatoes
- 2 cups homemade chicken stock
- 1 tablespoon olive oil
- 1 sweet onion, minced
- ½ teaspoon thyme
- Dash of sea salt and ground black pepper

Directions:

1. Heat the olive oil in a saucepan over medium-high flame. Add the onions, thyme and sweet potatoes and sauté for 10 minutes.

2. Pour the stock, coconut milk and coconut cream into the saucepan and stir. Let the soup simmer for 10 minutes.

3. Add the tilapia fillets into the chowder then season the dish with salt and pepper. Continue cooking the chowder for 5 minutes then turn off the flame.

4. Pour the soup into individual bowls and serve immediately.

5. This recipe yields 5 servings.

DINNER

Garlic-Infused Roast Beef

Ingredients:

- 700 grams beef roast

- 2 teaspoons dried rosemary

- 5 garlic cloves, chopped

- 2 tablespoons olive oil

- ½ teaspoon sea salt

- ½ teaspoon ground black pepper

Directions:

1. Preheat the oven to 350°F.

2. Using a knife, make small slits around the roast then place chopped garlic into each opening. Rub the roast with salt, pepper, rosemary and olive oil.

3. Lay the roast in a baking dish and pierce a cooking thermometer into the meat. Bake the roast beef in the oven until an internal temperature of 160° F is reached.

4. Let the roast beef cool at room temperature for 10 minutes before slicing it.

5. This recipe yields 6 servings.

SNACK

Zucchini Brownies

Ingredients:

- 2 cups shredded zucchini

- 1 cup almond butter

- ½ cup maple syrup

- 1 cup dark chocolate chips

- 1 large egg, whisked

- 1 teaspoon cinnamon powder

- 1 teaspoon vanilla extract

- 1 teaspoon baking soda

Directions:

1. Preheat the oven to 350°F and prepare a 9x9 baking dish greased with a little olive oil.

2. Combine zucchini, almond butter, maple syrup, chocolate chips, cinnamon powder, vanilla extract and baking soda in a bowl and mix well. Pour the brownie mixture into the baking pan.

3. Bake the brownies in the oven for 50 minutes or until a pierced toothpick comes out clean. Slice the brownies into 12 portions and serve warm.

4. This recipe yields 12 servings.

DAY 20

BREAKFAST

Detoxifying Green Juice

Ingredients:

- 2 cups spinach leaves

- 1 whole orange, peeled and deseeded

- 2 cups chopped celery

- 1 bunch parsley, chopped

- 2 cups chopped mangoes

- 1 cup chopped cucumber

- 2 bananas, chopped

- 1 cup lemon juice

- 1 cup lime juice

- 2 tablespoons raw honey

- 4 cups water

Directions:

1. Place 2 cups of water, parsley and spinach leaves in a blender and pulse. Add in bananas, celery and cucumber then mix for 20 seconds.

2. Gradually pour in the mangoes, oranges, lemon juice, lime juice, honey and remaining water into the blender. Mix the juice for 30 seconds then pour into individual glasses. Serve immediately.

3. This recipe yields 4 servings.

LUNCH

Quick and Easy Baked Eggs

Ingredients:

- 6 large eggs

- 1 large tomato, chopped

- 1 teaspoon olive oil

- 1 cup frozen spinach, thawed

- 5 tablespoons cottage cheese

- 2 tablespoons almond milk

- Pinch of sea salt and ground black pepper

Directions:

1. Preheat the oven to 350°F and grease a round baking dish with olive oil.

2. Arrange the spinach randomly inside the dish. Crack the eggs into the baking dish, making sure to not break them.

3. Pour in the almond milk then sprinkle tomatoes, cottage cheese, salt and pepper.

4. Place the dish in the oven and bake for 15 minutes. Let the baked eggs cool for 5 minutes. Use a knife and spatula to transfer the baked eggs to individual plates.

5. This recipe yields 3 servings.

DINNER

Crockpot Beef Fajitas

Ingredients:

- 600 grams chuck steak

- 2 red bell peppers, deseeded and julienned

- ¼ cup water

- 1 small onion, chopped

- ½ teaspoon paprika

- ½ teaspoon cayenne pepper

- ½ teaspoon garlic powder

- 1 teaspoon sea salt

- 1 teaspoon chili powder

- ½ teaspoon dried oregano

- ½ teaspoon cumin

Directions:

1. Place the beef into a 4-quart crockpot. Add in peppers, water, onions, paprika, cayenne pepper, garlic powder, sea salt, chili powder, oregano and cumin.

2. Cover the pot and cook the fajitas on low for 7-8 hours.

3. Shred the beef with a fork and mix with the sauce inside the pot. Transfer the fajitas to dinner plates and serve immediately.

4. This recipe yields 6 servings.

SNACK

Tropical Papaya Popsicles

Ingredients:

- 2 cups diced papaya, deseeded

- 2 cups full-fat coconut milk

- 2 teaspoons lemon juice

- 1 tablespoon maple syrup

Directions:

1. Place the papaya chunks in a food processor and puree until smooth. Add in the lemon juice, maple syrup and coconut milk. Blend the ingredients until a creamy texture is produced.

2. Gradually pour the papaya blend into 4 popsicle molds and freeze them for 5 hours. Serve frozen.

3. This recipe yields 4 servings.

DAY 21

BREAKFAST

Rosemary and Thyme Pork Sausages

Ingredients:

- 1½ kilograms lean ground pork

- 2 teaspoons dried rosemary

- 4 teaspoons fresh thyme

- 2 tablespoons chopped green onions

- 2 eggs, whisked

- 1 tablespoon sea salt

- 1 tablespoon maple syrup

- 1 teaspoon ground black pepper

- 1 teaspoon Dijon mustard

- 2 tablespoons olive oil

Directions:

1. Combine ground pork, eggs, rosemary, thyme and green onions in a bowl. Use a wooden spoon to mix the ingredients then season with salt, pepper, mustard and maple syrup. Stir until well-combined.

2. Use your hands to make 20 round patties from the sausage mixture. Set aside.

3. Heat the oil in a large pan over medium-high flame. Place the patties on the pan and cook each side for 5-7 minutes. Do this in 3 to 4 batches.

4. This recipe yields 10 servings.

Cold Tabbouleh Salad

Ingredients:

- 2 tablespoons chopped mint leaves

- 2 cups grated cauliflower

- 1 ½ cups finely-chopped tomatoes

- ½ cup chopped fresh parsley

- 1 teaspoon sea salt

- 2 tablespoons lemon juice

- ½ cup olive oil

- ½ teaspoon ground black pepper

Directions:

1. Whisk together olive oil, lemon juice, salt and black pepper. Add in mint leaves, cauliflower, tomatoes and parsley. Slowly mix the salad until well-combined.

2. Place the salad in the fridge for 2 hours. This salad is best served cold.

3. This recipe yields 3 servings.

DINNER

Hot and Spicy Lamb Skewers

Ingredients:

- 800 grams lamb meat, cut into 1-inch pieces

- 3 tablespoons olive oil

- 1 teaspoon dried oregano

- 1 tablespoon ground cumin

- 2 tablespoons apple cider vinegar

- 1 teaspoon ground coriander

- ¼ teaspoon chili powder

- 1 tablespoon minced garlic

- 1 tablespoon ground black pepper

- 1 tablespoon raw honey

- Metal skewers

Directions:

1. Combine olive oil, oregano, cumin, vinegar, coriander, chili powder, garlic, pepper and honey in a large bowl and mix well.

2. Mix in the lamb chunks and toss. Marinade the lamb in the spices overnight.

3. Thread the lamb on metal skewers. Grill the lamb on the grill for 5 minutes, flip them over then continue grilling for another 5 minutes. Serve immediately.

4. This recipe yields 6 servings.

SNACK

Thyme Sweet Potato Fries

Ingredients:

- 2 large sweet potatoes, peeled and julienned
- ½ teaspoon cinnamon powder
- 1 teaspoon fresh thyme leaves
- 1 tablespoon olive oil
- 1 teaspoon garlic powder
- Pinch of sea salt

Directions:

1. Preheat the oven to 375°F and line a baking sheet with parchment paper.

2. Place the sweet potatoes in a bowl and pour olive oil all over the vegetables. Season the sweet potatoes with cinnamon powder, salt, garlic powder and thyme. Toss the ingredients together.

3. Arrange the coated sweet potatoes on the baking sheet then place it in the oven. Bake them for 30-40 minutes or until the fries turn golden. Let it cool on a wire rack for 10 minutes. Serve warm.

4. This recipe yields 4 servings.

Chapter 7: Week 4 Recipes

DAY 22

BREAKFAST

Spiced Apple Oatmeal

Ingredients:

- 2 apples, peeled, cored and pureed

- 2 cups water

- 1 cup coconut milk

- 1 cup steel cut oats

- 1 teaspoon cinnamon

- 1 tablespoon raw honey

- 1 teaspoon vanilla extract

- Chopped almonds

Directions:

1. Combine water, coconut milk, oats and vanilla in a saucepan over medium-high flame. Stir the ingredients then allow it to simmer for 3-5 minutes.

2. Lower the flame to medium then mix in honey and cinnamon. Cook for 1 minute.

3. Pour in the pureed apples and stir. Cook for 1 minute then turn off the heat. Spoon the oatmeal into smaller bowls and top with chopped almonds. Serve immediately.

4. This recipe yields 4 servings.

5.

LUNCH

Roasted Bok Choy Salad

Ingredients:

- 4 pieces Bok Choy, halved

- 2 tablespoons olive oil

- 1 teaspoon Dijon mustard

- 2 tablespoons balsamic vinegar

- 2 tablespoons coconut aminos

- 1 tablespoon sesame oil

- ½ teaspoon powdered ginger

- 2 garlic cloves, minced

- 1 teaspoon paprika

- Pinch of sea salt and ground black pepper

Directions:

1. Pour olive oil on the Bok Choy halves, making sure to reach the leaves at the center. Grill the Bok Choy for 5 minutes, sliced part facing down.

2. While the vegetables are grilling, whisk together mustard, vinegar, coconut aminos, sesame oil, ginger, garlic, paprika, salt and pepper. Set aside the salad dressing.

3. Flip the Bok Choy over and grill the remaining side for 4 minutes. Transfer the grilled vegetables on a serving plate then drizzle the salad dressing on top. Serve warm.

DINNER

Gluten-Free Breaded Chicken

Ingredients:

- 2 large chicken breasts

- 2 cups almond flour

- ½ cup grated coconut

- 1 tablespoon coconut milk

- 2 large eggs, whisked

- ½ teaspoon white pepper

- 1 teaspoon sea salt

- 2 tablespoons olive oil

Directions:

1. Slice the chicken breast by cutting through the center of the meat without cutting the breast in half completely. Use a kitchen mallet to pound the breast and flatten it.

2. Whisk together eggs and milk then soak the chicken breasts in the mixture. Let the chicken marinade in the egg mixture for 2 hours.

3. Mix the pepper, salt, almond flour and coconut in a bowl. Coat the marinated chicken with the flour mixture.

4. Heat the oil in a pan over medium-high flame. Fry each side of the chicken breast for 5 minutes. Lay the chicken on a bed of paper towels to drain excess oil.

5. This recipe yields 4 servings.

SNACK

Freezer-Friendly Green Soup

Ingredients:

- 350 grams spinach leaves

- 1 cauliflower head, chopped

- 1 tablespoon chopped garlic

- 1 small white onion, minced

- 4 cups homemade chicken stock

- 1 cup coconut milk

- 1 teaspoon olive oil

- Dash of sea salt

Directions:

1. Heat the olive oil in a medium saucepan over medium-high flame. Cook the garlic and onions for 5 minutes.

2. Add in the spinach leaves and sauté for 5 minutes. Once the leaves have wilted, mix in the cauliflower, coconut milk, salt and chicken stock. Stir the soup ingredients then cover the saucepan.

3. Let the soup simmer for 10 minutes or until the cauliflower is tender. Turn off the heat and uncover the pot.

4. Place an immersion blender into the soup and blend until the mixture becomes creamy. Let the soup cool completely.

5. Once the soup has cooled down, transfer it to an airtight container and place it in the freezer where it can last for 1 month. This soup is best served cold.

6. This recipe yields 6 servings.

DAY 23

BREAKFAST

Blueberry and Peach Smoothie

Ingredients:

- 2 cups blueberries, frozen overnight
- 1 cup pureed peaches
- ½ cup fresh lemon juice
- 1 cup flaxseed meal
- 2 cups almond milk

Directions:

1. Place the blueberries, peaches, lemon juice, flaxseed meal and almond milk in a food processor. Blend for 30 seconds then pour into individual glasses. Serve immediately.

2. This recipe yields 5 servings.

LUNCH

Cajun Pork Stew

Ingredients:

- 5 pork chops, deboned and trimmed
- ½ tablespoon chili powder
- ½ tablespoon paprika
- ½ tablespoon cayenne
- ½ tablespoon coriander
- 3 cups cherry tomatoes, halved
- 2 medium zucchinis, chopped
- 1 red onion, chopped
- 1 tablespoon olive oil

Directions:

1. Preheat the oven to 250°F and prepare 2 baking dishes greased with equal amount of the olive oil.

2. Place the tomatoes, zucchini and onions in one baking dish. Set aside.

3. Mix together the chili powder, paprika, cayenne and coriander. Rub the spice mixture on all sides of the pork chops.

4. Lay the pork chops in a separate baking dish then place it in the oven. Bake for 15 minutes.

5. Open the oven then flip the pork chops over. Place the baking dish with the vegetables in the oven. Bake the meat and vegetables for 15 minutes.

6. Remove both dishes from the oven. Arrange the pork chops and roasted vegetables on a serving dish. Pour all of the remaining liquids from the pan onto the pork chops. Serve immediately.

7. This recipe yields 5 servings.

DINNER

Summer Waldorf Salad

Ingredients:

- 2 red apples, cored and sliced

- 3 celery stalks, chopped

- 2 cups shredded Romaine lettuce

- 2 tablespoons lemon juice

- ½ cup chopped almonds

- 2 tablespoons organic mayonnaise

- ½ cup chopped red onions

- Pinch of sea salt

Directions:

1. Whisk together mayonnaise, lemon juice and salt. Add in apples, celery, lettuce, red onions and almonds. Toss the salad ingredients.

2. Place the salad in the fridge for 1 hour. Serve immediately.

3. This recipe yields 3 servings.

SNACK

Cinnamon Butternut Crisps

Ingredients:

- 1 400- gram butternut squash, peeled and deseeded

- ½ teaspoon cinnamon powder

- ¼ teaspoon nutmeg

- ¼ teaspoon powdered ginger

- 2 tablespoons olive oil

- ½ teaspoon sea salt

- 1 tablespoon honey

Directions:

1. Preheat the oven to 250°F and prepare a parchment-lined baking sheet.

2. Use a mandolin to slice the butternut squash into thin chips. Place the squash pieces in a bowl and set aside.

3. In a separate bowl, mix together cinnamon powder, nutmeg, ginger, salt and olive oil. Pour the spice mixture into the squash chips and toss them together.

153

4. Arrange the squash chips on the baking sheet. Bake the chips in the oven for 1 hour or until they turn crispy. Let the chips cool on a wire rack for 15 minutes.

5. Drizzle honey all over the chips then serve immediately.

6. This recipe yields 4 servings.

DAY 24

BREAKFAST

Cheesy Tomato & Lettuce Wraps

Ingredients:

- ½ cup cottage cheese

- 4 iceberg lettuce leaves

- 4 romaine lettuce leaves, chopped

- 4 slices bacon, cooked and chopped

- 1 large tomato, deseeded and chopped

- 2 tablespoons coconut cream

- 2 teaspoons lemon juice

- Pinch of sea salt and ground black pepper

Directions:

1. Whisk together the coconut cream and lemon juice. Add in romaine lettuce, bacon, chopped tomatoes, salt and ground black pepper. Mix well

2. To assemble each wrap, place a piece of iceberg lettuce on a plate. Spoon the romaine and tomato mixture into leaf and roll. Do the same procedure for the remaining ingredients. Serve immediately.

3. This recipe yields 2 servings.

LUNCH

Lime Shrimp Skewers

Ingredients:

- 25 pieces shrimp, peeled and deveined

- 3 tablespoons lime juice

- ¼ teaspoon sea salt

- 3 tablespoons olive oil

- ½ teaspoon dried oregano

- 2 garlic cloves, minced

- ½ teaspoon dried thyme

- Pinch of ground black pepper

- Metal skewers

Directions:

1. Combine lime juice, sea salt, olive oil, oregano, garlic, thyme and black pepper in a bowl. Add in the shrimp then toss. Place the bowl inside the fridge and let the seafood marinade for 3 hours.

2. Take out the marinated shrimp for the fridge. Thread 5 pieces of shrimp per skewer then place it on a hot grill. Grill each side for 3 minutes.

3. Squeeze fresh lime juice on each shrimp skewer and serve immediately.

DINNER

5-Spice Crockpot Pork Ribs

Ingredients:

- 700 grams pork ribs

- 1 teaspoon cinnamon powder

- 1 tablespoon garlic powder

- 1 tablespoon grated ginger

- 1 teaspoon ground allspice

- ½ teaspoon ground black pepper

- ½ cup raw honey

- ½ cup coconut aminos

- ½ cup water

- 2 tablespoons chopped fresh parsley

Directions:

1. Arrange the pork ribs inside the crockpot. Pour in water, honey and coconut aminos.

2. Combine cinnamon powder, garlic powder, ginger, allspice and pepper in a bowl. Pour the spice mixture into the pork ribs then cover the pot.

3. Cook the ribs on high for 4 hours. Transfer the ribs to a serving dish and sprinkle chopped parsley on top.

4. This recipe yields 6 servings.

5.

SNACK

High-Fiber Chocolate Milkshake

Ingredients:

- 3 cups water

- 6 tablespoons cocoa powder

- ¾ cup coconut cream

- 3 tablespoons ground chia seeds

- 4 tablespoons coconut oil

- ½ teaspoon almond extract

- ½ teaspoon chili powder

- 3 tablespoons raw honey

- 1 cup ice

Directions:

1. Place cocoa powder, chia seeds, coconut oil, almond extract, chili powder and honey in a blender and pulse. Pour in the water and ice then mix for 30 seconds.

2. Pour the milkshake in individual glasses and serve immediately.

3. This recipe yields 4 servings.

BREAKFAST

Spinach and Cherry Tomato Omelet

Ingredients:

- 6 large eggs

- 1 cup cherry tomatoes, halved

- ½ cup chopped green onions

- 1 cup spinach leaves

- 2 garlic cloves, crushed

- ½ tablespoon olive oil

- 1 teaspoon paprika

- Pinch of sea salt and ground black pepper

Directions:

1. Heat the oil in a pan over medium-high flame. Place garlic, tomatoes and spinach in the pan and cook for 7 minutes. Season the veggies with salt, pepper and paprika. Remove the cooked vegetables from the pan and set aside.

2. Pour the eggs into the pan and stir while cooking for 2 minutes. Once the eggs are almost set, pour the cooked veggies on one side of the omelet and let it set for 1 minute.

3. Use a spatula to flip the empty side of the egg over the veggies and press downwards. Cook for 1 minute. Slowly flip the omelet and cook the remaining side for 2 minutes.

4. Slide the omelet into a plate and slice into 3 even portions. Serve while hot.

5. This recipe yields 3 servings.

LUNCH

Crusty Dill Crab Cakes

Ingredients:

- 450 grams pre-cooked crabmeat, flaked

- 1 large egg

- 3 tablespoons minced green bell pepper

- 3 green onions, minced

- 3 teaspoons fresh dill

- 1 tablespoon Dijon mustard

- 1½ cups almond flour

- Pinch of sea salt and ground black pepper

- 2 tablespoons olive oil

Directions:

1. Place the crabmeat, 1 cup almond flour, egg, bell pepper, onions, dill, mustard, salt and pepper in a food processor and mix for 20 seconds.

2. Transfer the mixture into a bowl and form 6 crab cake patties. Place the patties on a baking sheet and chill it in the fridge for 1 hour.

3. After 1 hour, take out the crab cakes from the fridge. Dredge them in the remaining almond flour then place it back on the sheet.

4. Heat the oil in a pan over medium-high flame. Pan-fry the crab cakes for 4 minutes on each side or until they turn golden brown. Serve immediately.

DINNER

Grilled Chicken and Brown Rice Bowl

Ingredients:

- 4 small chicken breast halves

- 2 tablespoons lemon pepper seasoning

- 2 cups cooked brown rice

- 1 cup shredded lettuce

- ½ yellow bell pepper, deseeded and julienned

- 1 cup rocket leaves

- 3 teaspoons lime juice

- 2 teaspoons olive oil

- Pinch of sea salt and ground black pepper

Directions:

1. Whisk together lime juice, olive oil, salt and pepper. Pour the dressing in a salad bowl together with lettuce, bell pepper and rocket. Toss then place the salad in the fridge.

2. Rub the lemon pepper seasoning on the chicken breasts and grill them for 8-10 minutes on each side. Let the chicken cool for 5 minutes. Slice each breast into 3 then set aside.

3. Remove the salad from the fridge. Mix in the cooked brown rice and toss them together. Spoon the rice and green salad into dinner plates and arrange the chicken slices on top. Serve immediately.

4. This recipe yields 4 servings.

SNACK

Spicy Baked Onion Rings

Ingredients:

- 3 white onions, peeled and sliced into rings

- ½ teaspoon ground black pepper

- ½ teaspoon paprika

- 1 ½ tablespoons olive oil

- ½ teaspoon pepper flakes

- 4 teaspoons grated Parmesan cheese

Directions:

1. Preheat the oven to 400°F and line a baking sheet with parchment paper.

2. Combine onions, pepper, paprika, pepper flakes and Parmesan in a bowl then toss. Pour in olive oil and toss the ingredients until the onion rings are well-coated.

3. Arrange the onions on the baking sheet and place it in the oven. Bake the onion rings for 10 minutes.

4. After 10 minutes, open the oven and flip the onions using long-handled tongs. Close the oven then bake the rings for another 10 minutes or until golden brown.

5. Place the baked onions on a wire rack and let it cool for 5 minutes. Serve immediately.

6. This recipe yields 6 servings.

DAY 26

BREAKFAST

Spiced Sweet Potato Flapjacks

Ingredients:

- 6 eggs, whisked

- 2 sweet potatoes, roasted and peeled

- 1 teaspoon cinnamon powder

- 1 tablespoon raw honey

- 1 teaspoon nutmeg

- 2 tablespoons olive oil

Directions:

1. Place the roasted sweet potatoes in a bowl and use a potato masher to mash the meat.

2. Mix in the eggs and honey. Season the batter with nutmeg and cinnamon powder then mix well.

3. Heat the oil in a pan over medium-high flame. Pour 2 tablespoons of the batter into the pan and let it cook for 5

minutes. Flip it over then cook the other side for another 5 minutes.

4. Place the cooked flapjacks on a plate and serve immediately.

5. This recipe yields 3-4 servings.

LUNCH

Mango, Cod, and Veggie Packets

Ingredients:

- 4 cod fillets

- 4 green onions, chopped

- 1 red bell pepper, deseeded and julienned

- 1 cup sliced carrots

- 1 cup sliced shiitake mushrooms

- 1 teaspoon olive oil

- 1 cup diced ripe mango

- 4 teaspoons coconut oil

- 2 tablespoons minced garlic

- Pinch of salt and ground black pepper

Directions:

1. Preheat the oven to 350°F and prepare 4 pieces of 24" x 20" aluminum foil sheets.

2. Heat the olive oil in a pan over medium flame. Cook the carrots, mushrooms and bell pepper for 5 minutes. Set aside.

3. Place each cod fillet on one side of an aluminum sheet. Top the fillet with garlic, salt, pepper, a teaspoon of coconut oil, green onions, mangoes and the cooked vegetables. Fold the empty side over the fish then seal the sides of the foil.

4. Place the foil packets on a baking dish. Bake for 30 minutes.

5. Carefully open the foil packets. Transfer the contents to a smaller dish then serve immediately.

6. This recipe yields 4 servings.

DINNER

Crockpot Leg of Lamb

Ingredients:

- 1 3-pound lamb leg

- 4 garlic cloves, minced

- 5 mint leaves, chopped

- 3 tablespoons coconut oil

- 5 cups chopped zucchini

- ½ cup chicken stock

- 1 teaspoon sea salt

- 1 teaspoon ground black pepper

Directions:

1. Heat the coconut oil in a large pot. Place the lamb leg inside the pot and sear the sides until brown. Transfer the lamb into a large crockpot.

2. Place the mint leaves and garlic on top of the lamb. Pour in the stock then cover the pot.

3. Cook the lamb on low temperature for 6 hours. After 6 hours, add the chopped zucchini into the pot then cover it. Cook for an extra 2 hours or until the lamb is tender.

4. This recipe yields 4 servings.

SNACK

Minty Melon Smoothie

Ingredients:

- 1 ½ cups cantaloupe, deseeded and chopped

- 1 ½ cups honeydew, deseeded and chopped

- 1 medium cucumber, peeled and chopped

- 1 small green apples, cored, peeled and chopped

- 4 mint leaves, chopped

- 1 cup chopped kale leaves

- 2 cups almond milk

- 1 tablespoon raw honey

- 1 cup ice cubes

Directions:

1. Place the cantaloupe, honeydew, cucumber, apples, kale and mint leaves in a blender and pulse.

2. Add in the honey, ice cubes and almond milk. Blend the smoothie until the desired consistency is reached.

3. Pour into glasses and serve immediately.

4. This recipe yields 3 servings.

DAY 27

BREAKFAST

Sunny Papaya Smoothie

Ingredients:

- 1 medium ripe papaya, peeled and deseeded

- 1 tablespoon fresh lemon juice

- 1 small apple, cored and peeled

- 1 cup coconut milk

Directions:

1. Slice the papaya into cubes and place in a food processor. Add in the apple, lemon juice and coconut milk.

2. Blend the ingredients until smooth and creamy. Pour into glasses and serve immediately.

3. This recipe yields 2 servings.

LUNCH

Egg and Sweet Potato Bowl

Ingredients:

- 4 eggs

- 3 bacon slices, chopped

- 4 cups grated sweet potatoes

- 1 small onion, minced

- ½ cup chopped fresh parsley

- ½ teaspoon sea salt

- ½ teaspoon paprika

- Pinch of ground black pepper

Directions:

1. Place the chopped bacon in a skillet over high flame. Cook the bacon until brown then add onions into the pan. Cook for 2 minutes.

2. Lower the flame to medium. Add sweet potatoes, parsley, salt, pepper and paprika into the pan and stir. Cover then let it cook for 8 minutes.

3. After 8 minutes, uncover the skillet and stir the sweet potato hash. Create 4 hollow wells in the potato mixture. Break an egg into each well and cover the skillet. Let the eggs cook for 5 minutes.

4. Place the hot skillet on a wooden chopping board and serve immediately.

5. This recipe yields 4 servings.

DINNER

Peppered Beef Tenderloin

Ingredients:

- 2 beef tenderloin steaks, fat trimmed off

- 3 teaspoons olive oil

- ¼ teaspoon sea salt

- ½ teaspoon crushed black peppercorns

- ¼ teaspoon white pepper

- ¼ teaspoon cayenne pepper

Directions:

1. Place the tenderloin in a bowl then drizzle half of the olive oil all over the meat. Sprinkle salt, peppercorns, white pepper and cayenne pepper onto the steaks and rub until all sides are evenly-coated.

2. Heat the remaining olive oil in a pan over medium-high flame. Place the steaks on the pan and fry for 3 minutes. Flip them over and cook the remaining side for another 3 minutes.

3. Transfer the steaks on a cooling rack and let it rest for 10 minutes. Slice the steaks then place them on a serving dish.

4. This recipe yields 2 servings.

SNACK

Low-Carb Lettuce and Tuna Salad

Ingredients:

- 1 ½ cups canned tuna in water, drained

- ½ romaine lettuce, finely chopped

- 2 teaspoons Dijon mustard

- ½ cup Greek yoghurt

- 1 tablespoon lemon juice

- 2 tablespoons sour cream

- Dash of sea salt

Directions:

1. Place the tuna in a bowl and flake it with a fork. Mix in lettuce, mustard, yoghurt, sour cream, lemon juice and salt. Toss the salad then place it in the fridge for 1 hour.

2. Transfer the salad to smaller bowls and serve cold.

3. This recipe yields 4 servings.

DAY 28

BREAKFAST

Stir-Fried Rice and Vegetables

Ingredients:

- 1 cup frozen peas and carrots, thawed

- 2 cups whole-grain brown rice, pre-cooked

- 1 cup sliced button mushrooms

- 2 eggs, beaten

- 1 tablespoon garlic powder

- 1 tablespoon olive oil

- Pinch of sea salt and ground black pepper

Directions:

1. Heat the olive oil in a pan over medium-high flame. Sauté the mushrooms for 3 minutes then add the peas, carrots, brown rice and garlic powder. Stir-fry the ingredients for 5 minutes while seasoning it with salt and pepper.

2. Add in the whisked eggs then continue cooking. Cover the pan and let the rice dish cook for 5-7 minutes.

3. Transfer the rice on a plate and serve immediately.

4. This recipe yields 4 servings.

LUNCH

Rosemary Turkey with Heirloom Vegetables

Ingredients:

- 2 large turkey breasts, halved

- 2 teaspoons fresh rosemary leaves

- 3 garlic cloves, crushed

- 2 tablespoons chopped fresh parsley

- Dash of sea salt and ground black pepper

- 2 cups chopped carrots

- 2 cups cherry tomatoes, halved

- 2 cups pearl onions, halved

- 2 teaspoons olive oil

Directions:

1. Preheat the oven to 400°F and prepare a roasting rack placed inside a roasting pan.

2. Combine rosemary leaves, salt, pepper, parsley and garlic in a bowl and mix well. Add the turkey breast into the bowl and rub the spices around the bird.

3. Place the turkey breasts on the roasting rack. Bake the turkey in the oven for 20 minutes.

4. After 20 minutes, place the carrots, tomatoes, onions and oil in the roasting pan and stir. Close the oven then lower the temperature to 350°F. Continue roasting the turkey and vegetables for 75 minutes.

5. Turn off the flame them remove the roasting rack and pan from the oven. Spoon the vegetables around the sides of the serving dish then place the turkey breasts in the middle. Serve hot.

6. This recipe yields 4 servings.

DINNER

Lettuce and Pear Salad with Raisins

Ingredients:

- 4 cups shredded Romaine lettuce leaves

- 3 pears, peeled, cored and julienned

- ½ cup golden raisins

- 1 small red onion, chopped

- ½ cup cottage cheese

- 2 tablespoons apple cider vinegar

- 2 tablespoons olive oil

- ½ teaspoon sea salt

- ¼ teaspoon ground black pepper

- 1 teaspoon raw honey

Directions:

1. To make the dressing, whisk together honey, apple cider vinegar, olive oil, salt and pepper. Set aside.

2. Combine lettuce, pears, raisins and red onion in a salad bowl then mix. Pour in cottage cheese and prepared dressing then toss the ingredients together.

3. Place the salad in the fridge for 1 hour. This salad is best served cold.

4. This recipe yields 4 servings.

SNACK

Blueberry Spinach Smoothie

Ingredients:

- 4 cups blueberries

- 6 cups spinach leaves, chopped

- 3 tablespoons almond butter

- 3 cups almond milk

- ½ cup flaxseed meal

- 1 tablespoon raw honey

Directions:

1. Combine blueberries, spinach, almond butter, almond milk, flaxseed and honey in a blender and mix until smooth and creamy.

2. Pour the drink into glasses and serve immediately.

3. This recipe yields 4 servings.

Chapter 8: Week 5 Recipes

DAY 29

BREAKFAST

Whole Wheat Crepes with Almond Butter

Ingredients:

- 3 large eggs, whisked

- 1 cup almond milk

- ¾ cup water

- 1 teaspoon almond extract

- 1 tablespoon coconut oil, melted

- 1 tablespoon raw honey

- 1 cup whole wheat flour

- 4 tablespoons almond butter

- Pinch of sea salt

Directions:

1. Combine eggs, almond milk, water almond extract, honey, flour and salt in a blender and process for 20 seconds. Set aside.

2. Heat the coconut oil in a non-stick pan over medium flame. Pour the crepe batter on the middle of the pan and constantly tilt it. This will allow the batter to spread thinly towards the sides.

3. Once the sides of the crepe start to loosen and turn brown, slowly flip the crepe over and cook the other side for 1-2 minutes.

4. Place the cooked crepe on a plate. Scoop a tablespoon of the almond butter then place it at the middle of the crepe. Roll or fold the crepe then serve.

5. This recipe yields 4-5 servings.

LUNCH

Vegetarian Broccoli Patties

Ingredients:

- 5 cups broccoli florets

- 1 cup pre-cooked quinoa

- 1 large egg, whisked

- 1 tablespoon minced garlic

- 1 tablespoon minced onion

- ½ cup shredded Parmesan cheese

- ¾ cup almond flour

- 2 tablespoons chopped parsley

- 2 tablespoons olive oil

- Dash of sea salt and ground black pepper

Directions:

1. Boil the broccoli in salted water for 6-8 minutes. Drain completely then place the vegetables in a food processor.

2. Mix in the egg, quinoa, Parmesan, flour, parsley, salt and pepper. Process the ingredients in the food processor for 20 seconds.

3. Pour the broccoli patty mixture in a bowl. Form 10-12 patties by rolling the mixture into balls and flattening them with your palms. Heat the olive oil in a pan over high flame and cook both sides of the patties until golden brown. Do this in two or three batches.

4. This recipe yields 5-6 servings.

DINNER

Ribeye Steak with Salad Greens

Ingredients:

- 2 large ribeye steaks, halved

- 2 tablespoons coconut oil

- 1 teaspoon sea salt

- 1 teaspoon ground black pepper

- 1 teaspoon garlic powder

- 1 teaspoon paprika

- 3 cups chopped romaine lettuce

- ½ cucumber, julienned

- ½ cup chopped green onions

- 3 tablespoons olive oil

- 2 tablespoons lemon juice

Directions:

1. To make the salad, toss together the lettuce, green onions, cucumber, 1 tablespoon olive oil and lemon juice. Place the salad in the fridge and chill until the steak is ready.

2. Preheat the oven to 275°F and prepare a foil-lined baking sheet with a wire rack on top of it.

3. Season the steaks with salt, pepper, garlic powder and paprika. Arrange the steaks on the wire rack then place the whole baking sheet with the steaks in the oven. Bake the steaks for 20 minutes or until the temperature of the meat reaches 40°C.

4. Heat the remaining olive oil in a pan over high heat. Brown each side of the steak for 2 minutes then let it cool on the wire rack for 10 minutes.

5. Place a piece of ribeye on a plate then serve it with a side of chilled salad greens.

6. This recipe yields 4 servings.

SNACK

Fruity Yoghurt with Toasted Coconut

Ingredients:

- 4 cups plain yoghurt

- 4 cups chopped mangoes

- ¼ cup ground almonds

- ¾ cup shredded coconut

- 1 tablespoon maple syrup

Directions:

1. Place the shredded coconut in an oven toaster and let it toast for 4 minutes.

2. Combine yoghurt, ground almonds and maple syrup in a bowl and stir. Top the yoghurt with the mangoes and toasted coconut.

3. This recipe yields 4 servings.

DAY 30

BREAKFAST

Avocado and Peppers Scramble

Ingredients:

- 1 cup diced avocado meat

- 3 eggs

- ½ cup chopped green bell pepper

- ½ teaspoon cayenne pepper

- 2 tablespoons grated Parmesan cheese

- 1 tablespoon olive oil

Directions:

1. Whisk together eggs and Parmesan cheese. Set aside.

2. Heat the olive oil in a skillet over medium-high flame. Cook the bell peppers for 2 minutes then pour in the egg mixture. Scramble the eggs while cooking, allowing the eggs to set.

3. Once the scrambled eggs are ready, transfer it to a plate. Top the eggs with the diced avocado and cayenne pepper. Serve immediately.

4. This recipe yields makes 2 servings.

LUNCH

Slow-Cooked Beef Ribs

Ingredients:

- 6 pieces beef short ribs, 5 ounces each

- 1 tablespoon minced ginger

- 1 tablespoon minced garlic

- 2 teaspoons coconut oil

- 1 tablespoon coconut flour

- 2 tablespoons coconut aminos

- ½ cup lemon juice

- 1 cup homemade chicken stock

- ½ cup chopped green onions

- 1 tablespoon raw honey

- Pinch of sea salt and ground black pepper

Directions:

1. Combine ribs, salt, pepper and flour. Heat the oil in a pan over medium-high flame then sear the ribs until the sides turn brown. Place the ribs into the crockpot and set aside.

2. On the same pan, sauté the garlic, ginger and green onions for 3 minutes. Add in the lemon juice, honey and coconut aminos and continue stirring for 2 minutes. Pour in the chicken stock and allow it to simmer.

3. Once the stock mixture is simmering, pour it into the crockpot with the ribs. Cover the pot and set the temperature to low. Let the ribs cook for 7 hours.

4. After 7 hours, place the ribs on a serving dish. Pour the sauce into a small pan and let it reduce for 3-5 minutes. Drizzle the sauce over the ribs and serve.

5. This recipe yields 6 servings.

DINNER

Stir-Fried Paleo Rice Bowl

Ingredients:

- 1 large cauliflower head, cut into chunks

- 3 cups water

- 1 tablespoon olive oil

- 2 tablespoons sun-dried tomatoes

- 1 cup cherry tomatoes, halved

- 1 cup chopped green bell peppers

- ½ cup chopped button mushrooms

- 1 teaspoon garlic powder

- ½ teaspoon sea salt

- ½ teaspoon turmeric

- Dash of ground black pepper

Directions:

1. To make cauliflower rice, combine water and cauliflower chunks in a blender and process for 10 seconds or until the vegetable has been minced. Drain the water completely from the cauliflower rice. Set aside.

2. Heat the olive oil in a pan over medium-high flame. Cook the mushrooms for 3 minutes then add in the bell peppers, cherry tomatoes and sun-dried tomatoes. Stir-fry the vegetables for 5 minutes. Season the veggies with salt, pepper, turmeric and garlic powder.

3. Mix in the cauliflower rice and stir it with the vegetables. Cook for 5-10 minutes then turn off the heat.

4. Place the stir-fried rice on a dish and serve immediately.

5. This recipe yields 5 servings.

Green Strawberry Smoothie

Ingredients:

- 2 cups chopped strawberries

- 8 cups chopped kale leaves

- 2 cups chopped celery

- 4 cups almond milk

- 1 tablespoon minced ginger

- 2 ½ tablespoons maple syrup

- Pinch of cinnamon powder

- 1 cup crushed ice

Directions:

1. Combine strawberries, kale, celery, almond milk, ginger, maple syrup and cinnamon powder in a blender and pulse. Add in crushed ice and blend for 20 seconds.

2. Pour into individual glasses and serve immediately.

3. This recipe yields 4 servings.

Conclusion

I hope this book was able to help you adopt a healthier lifestyle by teaching you how to whip up delicious whole food recipes for yourself and your family.

The difficult journey towards weight loss is made easier by including whole foods in your diet. With fruits, vegetables, meats, oils, and other organic foods by your side, you will achieve your fitness goals faster and become more confident with your body.

The next step is to continue your weight loss journey by cooking more whole food recipes daily. It is time to expand your know-how on the health benefits of clean eating by reading books, websites, and other materials that promote appreciation for whole foods.

I wish you the best of luck!

Samantha Clare

Made in the USA
San Bernardino, CA
29 June 2016